Al-Ghazālī and the Idea of Moral Beauty

Al-Ghazālī and the Idea of Moral Beauty rethinks the relationship between the good and the beautiful by considering the work of eleventh-century Muslim theologian Abū Ḥāmid al-Ghazālī (d. 1111).

A giant of Islamic intellectual history, al-Ghazālī is celebrated for his achievements in a wide range of disciplines. One of his greatest intellectual contributions lies in the sphere of ethics, where he presided over an ambitious attempt to integrate philosophical and scriptural ideas into a seamless ethical vision. The connection between ethics and aesthetics turns out to be a signature feature of this account. Virtue is one of the forms of beauty, and human beings are naturally disposed to respond to it with love. The universal human response to beauty in turn provides the central paradigm for thinking about the love merited by God. While al-Ghazālī's account of divine love has received ample attention, his special way of drawing the good into relation with the beautiful has, oddly, escaped remark. In this book Sophia Vasalou addresses this gap by offering a philosophical and contextual study of this aspect of al-Ghazālī's ethics and of the conception of moral beauty that emerges from it.

This book will be of interest to scholars and students in Islamic ethics, Islamic intellectual history, and the history of ethics.

Sophia Vasalou is a Senior Lecturer in Philosophical Theology at the University of Birmingham. Her research focuses on philosophical and theological ethics in the Islamic world. Her published works include *Moral Agents and Their Deserts: The Character of Muʿtazilite Ethics* (2008), *Schopenhauer and the Aesthetic Standpoint: Philosophy as a Practice of the Sublime* (2013), and *Wonder: A Grammar* (2015).

Islam in the World

Series Editors:
Katherine Brown, Birmingham University, UK
Jorgen Nielsen, Birmingham University, UK

Freedom of Speech in Universities
Islam, Charities and Counter-terrorism
Alison Scott-Baumann and Simon Perfect

Rivals in the Gulf
Yusuf al-Qaradawi, Abdullah Bin Bayyah, and the Qatar-UAE Contest Over the Arab Spring and the Gulf Crisis
David H. Warren

Al-Ghazālī and the Idea of Moral Beauty
Sophia Vasalou

For more information and a full list of titles in the series, please visit: https://www.routledge.com/Islam-in-the-World/book-series/ITWF

Al-Ghazālī and the Idea of Moral Beauty

Sophia Vasalou

Routledge
Taylor & Francis Group
LONDON AND NEW YORK

First published 2022
by Routledge
2 Park Square, Milton Park, Abingdon, Oxon OX14 4RN

and by Routledge
605 Third Avenue, New York, NY 10158

Routledge is an imprint of the Taylor & Francis Group, an informa business

British Library Cataloguing-in-Publication Data
A catalogue record for this book is available from the British Library

Library of Congress Cataloging-in-Publication Data
A catalog record has been requested for this book

ISBN: 978-1-032-05205-2 (hbk)
ISBN: 978-1-032-05206-9 (pbk)
ISBN: 978-1-003-19655-6 (ebk)

DOI: 10.4324/9781003196556

Typeset in Times New Roman
by KnowledgeWorks Global Ltd.

Contents

Acknowledgements

I'm very grateful to the two reviewers for their careful reading and constructive suggestions, and to my colleague Katherine Brown for steering this work to publication. I'm also grateful to the audience at a talk I gave on the subject at the Oxford Centre for Islamic Studies for their questions and comments. The 2019 pandemic put paid to other opportunities to share this work live, but there are brighter days ahead.

1 Introduction

... would Eros be anything except love of beauty?

Plato, *Symposium*

At a celebrated juncture of the *Symposium*, Plato describes the ascending course an individual must trace through the different objects of love. From love of beautiful bodies, the lover will progress to love of beautiful souls, to love of beautiful laws, practices, and sciences, and finally to love of the transcendent form of Beauty itself, on which all mundane beauty depends (210a–212a).[1] Holding this piece of philosophical idealisation together are a number of important assumptions. The idea that souls can be beautiful or ugly is one. The idea that the beautiful and the good are inseparably connected is another; what makes a soul beautiful, to take a key example, is its virtues. Finally, there is the idea that the truest beauty is transcendent, and all particular beauty points to and depends on it. Some of these ideas pick out features that were central to the physiognomy of Platonic and Neoplatonic philosophy in particular. Yet some of them enjoy broader reach, representing features frequently taken to be integral to ancient philosophical and indeed non-philosophical thinking more generally. The connection between the beautiful and the good, most notably, is embedded in the basic facts of linguistic usage. "[I]n Hellenic culture," as one scholar has crystallised an oft-made observation, "the beautiful and the good are brought together in a single notion." That notion is the Greek term *to kalon*, which can refer equally to the kinds of things we would naturally call "beautiful" (such as human faces or bodies) and to the kinds of things we would naturally call "good" (such as human actions and traits).[2]

To contemporary philosophical sensibility, many of the features just listed have come to seem eccentric. The idea, in particular, that ethical considerations could intersect or even—in some manner still to be

DOI: 10.4324/9781003196556-1

defined—coincide with aesthetic ones is liable to appear intellectually indefensible if not morally pernicious. Despite certain structural similarities, such as the ostensible independence of both moral and aesthetic value from antecedent personal interests or purposes, these kinds of value would seem to be separated by a gulf. Aryeh Kosman articulates part of the ground of this concern when he remarks that

> we would find it decadent or something like belleletristic to be directed to keep a promise because it would be lovely or in good taste to do so, or enjoined not to commit mass murder because doing so would be tacky. For us, "she acted beautifully" and "she acted rightly" do not mean the same thing.

Put differently, moral reasons carry a type of normative demand that aesthetic considerations do not.[3]

Yet more recently, there has been a surge of philosophical efforts to bridge this perceived gulf. Taking their focus from the virtues and the vices, the most significant of these projects have set out to restore credibility to talk of beauty with reference to human character or the human soul. "Moral beauty," in the view of Panos Paris, is neither loose talk nor a category error, but perfectly in order when applied to the excellence of a person's character traits taken as complex forms that promote a particular end (the human good). Defending this view involves expanding the cramped conception of aesthetic objects that has come to dominate philosophical aesthetics, with art and nature, and by extension sensory objects, monopolising the discussion.[4]

Many of these philosophical projects are framed as attempts to honour our ordinary ways of thinking and talking about ethics, and about human character in particular. "We may call someone who exhibits many moral virtues a beautiful person," Berys Gaut points out, just as "we may say of a kind and generous action that it was a beautiful action." Colin McGinn lists a number of terms of approval and disapproval that he suggests have substantial aesthetic connotations, including "sweet" and "pure," "foul," "disgusting," "or "grotesque."[5] We can see these linguistic intuitions at work in prominent literary texts, as in Jane Eyre's admiring ascription of a "beauty neither of fine colour nor long eyelash, nor pencilled brow, but of meaning, of movement, of radiance" to one of the characters of the eponymous novel.[6] These intuitions unite us to the proximate past, as this literary example attests. The same applies to Gaut's expression, which echoes nothing more than Hume's remark, in the *Treatise*, that "[t]here is no spectacle so fair and beautiful as a noble and generous action."[7] The latter remark reflects a broader willingness among Hume and his contemporaries to reach for aesthetic language in speaking about qualities of character. Recent projects have thus also taken their bearings from philosophical history, both proximate (as represented by Hume and his peers) and remote (as represented by their ancient precursors), viewing their project as in part one of restoration.

In this work, my aim is to broaden the philosophical record to include an important episode that has not yet received adequate consideration. This is the episode contributed by the prominent eleventh-century Muslim theologian Abū Ḥāmid al-Ghazālī (d. 1111). Many of the ideas picked out on the previous page as central tropes of ancient philosophical thinking—particularly in the Platonic and Neoplatonic schools—turn out to have significant counterparts within the Islamic world. Partly, this is the result of intellectual influence, as ancient texts that formed key vectors of these ideas were translated into Arabic and found their way into the hands of Arabic-speaking intellectuals. That material process, it must be said, was not the most straightforward, and in certain regards, the textual links appear surprisingly thin. Plato's *Symposium*, for example, seems never to have been translated into Arabic, though some of its ideas made it into Arabic-Islamic culture through indirect routes, reflecting a generally patchy record of transmission for Plato's corpus as a whole. Plotinus' *Enneads*, in which these kinds of ideas achieved a critical articulation, was only available in part and in paraphrase under the title *The Theology of Aristotle*.[8] Yet a reasonable leaven of these philosophical ideas made it into the mix of intellectual elements at work in the Islamic world, and it entered into a variety of intellectual schemes that elaborated the relations between ethics, aesthetics, and metaphysics. This includes, above all, Sufism, where the idea of God's transcendent beauty—which worldly entities either naturally manifest or normatively seek to emulate—formed a cynosure of spiritual preoccupation.[9]

A thinker of boundless ambition, breadth, and curiosity, al-Ghazālī drew equally from the granary of philosophical and Sufi ideas in crafting his own intellectual vision. Both influences can be seen at work in his late-life multi-volume masterpiece, *The Revival of the Religious Sciences*, where this vision receives its most powerful and influential expression. Al-Ghazālī's purpose in this book is to guide the reader through the process of ethical and spiritual formation required to reach ultimate happiness, this being happiness in God. It is in this context that al-Ghazālī makes an approach to a theme that has formed the defining focus of Sufi spirituality, the love of God. This approach turns out to be an account of ethics, aesthetics, and metaphysics rolled into one. Love of God is love of beauty; and virtue is one of the forms of beauty.

Although al-Ghazālī's account of divine love in the *Revival* has justly received considerable attention, its special way of drawing the good into relation with the beautiful has oddly escaped remark.[10] One reason for wishing to focus attention on it, as already suggested, is to enrich the historical record we survey and seek to mine as we attempt to rethink the relationship between the good and the beautiful, ethics and aesthetics. If we believe this effort is worthwhile, a broadened sense of intellectual community will seem worth cultivating. But a closer meditation on this aspect of al-Ghazālī's thinking is also important if we are interested in gaining a clearer insight into al-Ghazālī's ethics on its own terms. Al-Ghazālī's ethics simply cannot be understood without taking into account the aesthetic framework in which he locates the ethical life, and more specifically the life of virtue. As I will show, the insight that results from this engagement is not entirely free from difficulty. Al-Ghazālī's account of the relation between the good and the beautiful turns out to problematise the unity of his thought, and to raise on fresh grounds an enigma familiar to his major interpreters concerning the consistency between the viewpoints of his different works. If we are to appreciate the complexity of al-Ghazālī's thought, and of Islamic ethical discourse more broadly, this is a challenge well worth confronting.

After a brief foray into al-Ghazālī's attitude to aesthetic enjoyment more generally (Section 2), I set out some of the linguistic, religious, and philosophical background that provides a context for al-Ghazālī's specific way of linking aesthetics with the domain of ethics (Section 3). I then begin to unpack the relation between the good and the beautiful as al-Ghazālī presents it in his key virtue-centred works, especially the *Revival*, focusing on the account of moral beauty he develops in the context of his discussion of the love of God (Section 4). Moral virtue is the prime exemplar of an intelligible type of beauty, and the disinterested love that human beings universally experience towards beauty provides the central paradigm for thinking about the love they may direct to God. Having explored this model philosophically, I then turn to consider the quandary it poses for our understanding of al-Ghazālī's oeuvre as a whole, given its apparent antagonism to the (anti-rationalist, anti-objectivist) view of ethical value expressed in his theological and legal works (Section 5). I try to meet this challenge by outlining a number of approaches that would allow us to remove the apparent contradiction, including appeals to chronology, levels of discourse, and "supercharged" hermeneutics (Section 6). A concluding comment (Section 7) tries to broaden the vista against which we engage with this particular episode and place the historical record in the service of the beautiful and the good.

2 The place of aesthetic experience in al-Ghazālī's ethics

A good way to get into our topic is through a broader question about the place of aesthetic experience in al-Ghazālī's thought. "Aesthetics"—from the Greek *aisthesis*, "sense" or "sense-perception"—is itself a modern concept with no exact counterpart in the medieval Islamic intellectual tradition. Aesthetics was not conceived of and pursued as a separate subject of inquiry. Yet beauty (*jamāl* or *ḥusn*) was a theme that preoccupied Muslim intelligentsia across numerous vehicles of cultural expression, including literature (*adab*), philosophy, and Sufism. In philosophy, beauty surfaced as a theme within discussions organised under rather different headings, such as metaphysical explorations of the nature of God or explorations of literary art inspired by Aristotle's *Rhetoric* and *Poetics*.[1] When we seek to study questions of "aesthetics" in a particular work or thinker, we will thus often need to track our subject through a variety of environments and to identify it using one or both of the following means: the use of core aesthetic vocabulary (such as *jamāl* and *ḥusn*) and the reference to experiences that *we* are happy to recognise as instances of the aesthetic in light of both their objects and their described phenomenology.[2]

Approaching al-Ghazālī in this manner, one of the first references to aesthetic experience we find in the *Revival of the Religious Sciences* will evoke an immediate sense of scepticism about the status of such experiences within his concerns. "Anyone who takes delight in the present world," he writes in the book *On the Condemnation of the Mundane World*, "be it by hearing some birdsong, by gazing upon some verdure (*khuḍra*), or by taking a drink of cool water, will have his reward in the hereafter diminished several times in proportion."[3] Both the objects and the broad phenomenology of these experiences allow us to confidently recognise them (at least the first two) as instances of aesthetic experience on our terms.[4] And al-Ghazālī's attitude to such experience seems unmistakably clear: it is one of thoroughgoing

DOI: 10.4324/9781003196556-2

condemnation. This ties in with the overall theme of the book, and the jaundiced attitude it adopts towards worldly goods and pleasures. There is a necessary disjunction, both psychological and evaluative, between attachment to goods that belong to the present world and attachment to goods that belong to the next. Attachment to the former comes at the cost of the latter; and on the level of our fundamental motivation and conception of the good, only one attachment can reign supreme.[5] To this ascetic view, there would appear to be no exceptions: all pleasures that form part of the worldly domain and are made possible by our embodied condition are tarred by the same brush, no matter whether they come to us through hearing and sight (honoured by Aristotle in the *Metaphysics* as the noblest and most intellectual of the senses) or through taste and feel. This includes the pleasures afforded by the most ordinary enjoyment of nature and natural beauty.

Yet in fact the attitude conveyed in this book does not tell the whole story. It may be evident that the above view, which tells us what should be our ultimate object of desire, leaves open a different way of valuing the goods and pleasures to be had in the present world. We may not value them intrinsically, but we may value them as goods that stand in a subordinate relation to the intrinsic goods of the supernatural realm. It is not, after all, that we should wholly reject the physical pleasures of eating and drinking. It is that when we partake of them, we should regard them under their description as means that enable us to realise our true end and that give us the power to devote ourselves to what really matters—to the salutary forms of intellectual and ethical activity (*al-ʿilm waʾl-ʿamal*). Seen in this light, eating and drinking become objects not merely of grudging toleration but of praise and reward (*mashkūr wa-maʾjūr*). For "the body is the vessel of the soul, which it uses to complete its journey toward God."[6] The present world is not an impediment to the next; it is the means of reaching it.

This way of regarding worldly objects finds its complement in a rather different mode of valuation. Entities belonging to the mundane realm may stand in a causal relationship to goods belonging to the metaphysical realm, which makes us value them in their instrumental capacity. Yet they may also stand in a signifying relationship to that realm, which makes us value them in their epistemic capacity and for their cognitive content. And it is a type of response to the natural world and its constituents we may recognise as aesthetic in character, being a response to its beauty and grandeur, that registers that relationship most strongly.

The best place to observe this attitude at work, in the *Revival*, is the book captioned *On Contemplation*. The contemplation in question has a number of different objects, but one of the most important consists in God's acts and effects as manifest in the created realm. Like all the other topics treated in the last quarter of the *Revival*, this contemplative exercise is not a recommended extra of the ethical life, but an activity we are dutybound to undertake if we are to achieve spiritual completeness. And this duty essentially takes shape as a duty of wonder, which reads every aspect of the created realm—from the components of our own bodies and the different plants and animals roaming land and sea to the larger economy of the heavens and the earth—as a wondrous signifier of God's attributes, above all his majesty, wisdom, knowledge, and power. It is possible that not all wonder has an aesthetic quality; but this kind of wonder certainly does. The mode of contemplation that reads the natural world as expressive of God's nature is one responsive to its grandeur and beauty. "You have forgotten," as al-Ghazālī observes in one place, "to have regard for the beauty of the empire of the heavens and the earth."[7]

So an aesthetic appreciation of the natural world is not only *not* reprehensible but mandated. But its legitimacy rests on our ability to experience the natural world as pointing to its transcendent cause. To return to the birdsong that antagonised al-Ghazālī in an earlier book of the *Revival*: it's not taking pleasure in birdsong that is problematic *simpliciter*; it's taking pleasure in birdsong *just* insofar as it's birdsong, and not insofar as it is a glorious expression of God's nature.

Whether we adopt one or the other of these two modes of valuation—instrumental or epistemic—may be a matter of perspective. The same object can provide the basis for both, as when we view the article of food we are consuming as a means to some valorised activity yet also as a token of the astounding natural economy God has created and as a signifier of God's beneficence and creative powers.[8]

Taken together, this shows that al-Ghazālī has a more nuanced attitude to aesthetic enjoyment. The positive attitude he displays towards the enjoyment of nature has its counterpart in the view he takes of certain forms of art. The most notable example is music, the subject of extensive controversy in the Islamic tradition. Al-Ghazālī is deeply impressed by the power of music, and by what our profound response to it says about our own nature and about the higher spiritual realities. Our response to music reveals the presence of a "divine spark" in us, and "beautiful, harmonious, well-proportioned sound produces an image of the wonders of that [higher spiritual] world."[9] As with nature, the value of music thus derives from the access it gives us, cognitive and emotional, to the transcendent realm, its beauty a reflection and conduit of transcendent beauty.

3 The good and/as the beautiful in context

Al-Ghazālī's more nuanced attitude to nature and certain forms of art thus provides an important corrective to the picture suggested by a partial reading of the *Revival*. Yet for the purposes of this investigation, even more interesting is the attitude towards aesthetic experience he displays in connection to ethics.

It is worth pausing over this contrast for moment in order to build some context. Professional philosophers studying aesthetics these days tend to focus on two broad types of objects as primary candidates for aesthetic response: nature and art. This focus is reflected among some of the founding figures of philosophical aesthetics, including Kant. Yet even in Kant's work, we find evidence of an interest in a different type of aesthetic object. This shows up less directly in his account of the beautiful than in his approach to the sublime, where in different locations and from different directions, he acknowledges that things that have moral content, to put it broadly, can evoke in the observer an experience of the sublime. The moral law can evoke that experience; so can awareness of our own moral vocation as human beings. The same applies to individuals who display certain kinds of exalted moral qualities. Thus, for example, "affectlessness (*apatheia, phlegma in significactu bono*) in a mind that emphatically pursues its own inalterable principles is sublime."[1] The kind of self-command in pursuit of the noble that Kant describes evokes the Stoic sage more narrowly, and a type of heroic outlook more broadly. A similar idea is expressed by Schopenhauer when he identifies his own version of "sublime character" as a distinctive object of aesthetic experience.[2]

The admiration we experience towards outstanding moral exemplars, this suggests, has an aesthetic modality—a modality that would on one level appear to be linked to the qualities of distance and elevation that define its object. Yet the association of the aesthetic and the ethical, as already mentioned, has a longer philosophical lineage. The world of

DOI: 10.4324/9781003196556-3

classical antiquity was the source not only of the prototypes that provide Kant and Schopenhauer with their models of the moral hero, but also of a broader way of conceptualising ethics that drew it into close connection with aesthetic ideas, as instanced, at the most fundamental level, by the Janus-faced nature of the Greek term *kalon*.

Just *how* that connection should be articulated—how exactly to understand the idea that "the beautiful and the good are brought together in a single notion," as phrased earlier—is still a matter for discussion. In a recent essay, for example, Terence Irwin has tried to redress a popular way of contrasting the type of connection between ethics and aesthetics we find among more recent philosophers—Kant and Schopenhauer, but also Hume, Smith, and Hutcheson—and the one at work among their Greek predecessors. Modern philosophers, even when they link the good and the beautiful in certain ways—whether by calling certain forms of character "sublime" (like Kant or Schopenhauer) or certain actions "fair and beautiful" (Hume), or by inquiring more generally into the relations between the good and the beautiful—are clear about the fact that they are inquiring "into two things rather than one."[3] Greek philosophers are thought to be different given the semantic profile of the term *kalon*. Yet Irwin's argument, framed relative to Aristotle, is that Aristotle makes a clear distinction between *kalon* in the sense of "morally right" and the sense of "beautiful," recognising these as two distinct properties. It is a mistake to suppose that he "ascribes one and the same property to all *kalon* things, or that he gives the same account of what makes them *kalon*. Some things are *kalon* insofar as they are beautiful, others insofar as they are well ordered, and others insofar as they are praiseworthy attempts to promote a common good." Hence there is "no good reason to claim that all *kalon* things are *kalon* insofar as they are beautiful. Aesthetic attractiveness belongs only to a proper subset of *kalon* things."[4] From a practical viewpoint, Irwin argues, these facts dictate that we should avoid translating *kalon* using different English terms and instead opt for a single term that accommodates both senses, such as "fine" or "admirable."

There are good reasons to dwell on this point, as we will see, though we will have to get to them in stages. We can start by observing that we find the same semantic profile in the core Arabic terms employed by al-Ghazālī and his contemporaries as we do in ancient Greek. Two of the key terms for "beauty," as mentioned earlier, are *jamāl* and *ḥusn*. Depending on their context, both of them can be translated with a range of terms that includes "good," "fine," or "beautiful."[5] Their commonest contrary, *qubḥ*, translates as both "bad" or "wrong" and "ugly." Both terms can be used to qualify and evaluate actions as well as traits of character. And both terms (sometimes with a slight morphological permutation) can be used to characterise the external appearance of objects or people. In a well-known hadith describing the Prophet's night journey (*isrāʾ*), both positive terms appear in apposition to qualify a beautiful woman (*imraʾa ḥasnāʾ jamlāʾ*). The close semantic relationship between these two terms is reflected in the works of several lexicographers and philologists. The eleventh-century language scholar al-Rāghib al-Iṣfahānī, for example, defines *jamāl* as an intensification of *ḥusn*, and he is followed by many of his successors.[6]

Significantly, the two terms are not equally dominant in different regions of Islamic ethical literature. In works of dialectical theology (*kalām*), it was the pair *ḥasan-qabīḥ* that lent its name to the notorious debates concerning the epistemic source and ontological status of ethical norms (are they known by religious scripture or human reason? Are they objective features or products of divine assignment?). In these debates, the focus was squarely on actions as objects of evaluative concern, and despite some residual awkwardness, in this context the pair of terms is often translated as "good-bad" or "right-wrong."[7] In theological texts of this sort, the term *jamīl* barely makes an appearance as a term of ethical evaluation.

Things look different in texts that betray the influence of Hellenistic civilisation and its philosophies. There, *jamīl* emerges as the dominant term of evaluation. This can be seen clearly, for example, in the Arabic translation of Galen's short but seminal text *Peri Ethon* (lost in the original Greek), which applies it to the virtues and the actions that derive from them.[8] It is *jamīl*, likewise, that usually translates *kalon* in Aristotle's *Nicomachean Ethics*, including in the context of the crucial distinction between the fine, the advantageous, and the pleasant (1104b31).[9] The resulting Arabic triad (*jamīl, nāfiʿ, ladhīdh*) would travel widely among works of philosophical and theological ethics receptive to the influence of the Hellenistic tradition. The prominence of the term *jamīl* would be reflected in these works, and for a number of writers, such as al-Fārābī (d. 950 or 951), it would form the chief evaluative currency.[10]

Thus, in ethical works where the conception of ethics centres on the virtues and bears an identifiable debt to the ancient philosophical tradition, the term *jamīl* occupies centre stage. The contribution of ancient philosophical texts, to be sure, went significantly beyond the mere shaping of terminological preference. A central component of their bequest lay in the substantive ideas they contributed to the intellectual conversation. Some of these ideas seem inseparable from issues of terminology: the limpid distinction between the fine and the advantageous is a good example (the moral world of a person who can enunciate that distinction is very different from the moral world of one who cannot). For our purposes, the most potent idea contributed by a number of these texts was the explicit application of the concept of beauty to the human soul, and the claim that beauty includes moral virtue as one of its most important forms.

This is an idea that appears openly in Galen's *Peri Ethon*. Having spoken of the fineness of actions and of people's love of the fine (*maḥabbat al-jamīl*), it goes on to compare the beauty (*jamāl*) of the soul to the beauty of the body, positing the same factor as the cause of both, namely, the realisation of a certain type of balance.[11] The balance in question in the former case is that between the different powers of the soul—appetitive, irascible, and rational—through which virtue is achieved. In discussing the beauty of the soul, we may note, the text uses the terms *jamāl* and *ḥusn* interchangeably.

Yet it is the work known as the *Theology of Aristotle*, representing a truncated and heavily edited translation of Plotinus' *Enneads*, that develops this theme in ways that would reverberate across different levels of Islamic intellectual culture. Distinguishing between the sensible and the intelligible world, the work locates the highest form of beauty (*ḥusn, jamāl, bahāʾ*) in the latter. True beauty should be sought in the interior (*bāṭin*) rather than the exterior (*ẓāhir, khārij*). One example of inner beauty is given to us by geometrical forms (*ṣuwar taʿlīmiyya*). But for our purposes, the most interesting case is the beauty constituted by the forms of human character. It is the "forms of the soul, such as magnanimity (*ḥilm*), dignity (*waqār*), and the like" that are truly beautiful (*ḥasana*). "When we find a person to be magnanimous and dignified, we wonder at his beauty (*ḥusn*) from this regard," even if his physical exterior is repellent (*qabīḥ*). Upright men (*al-marʾ al-ṣāliḥ*) and wise men endowed with intellect and knowledge captivate us and make us long to feast our gaze on them. This longing, the text suggests, is criterial of an aesthetic response: for an object to be beautiful is for it to arouse the desire to contemplate. And this is an invitation that both moral virtue and intellectual virtue extend.[12]

One feature that sets the adapted *Theology* apart from the original *Enneads*, as Peter Adamson has observed, is the strong ethical emphasis it introduces into various parts of the discussion.[13] This is reflected in its treatment of inner beauty as just outlined. Interestingly, this ethical emphasis would not be taken up to an equal degree by the wide range of Muslim intellectuals who proved permeable to the influence of these philosophical ideas, including al-Fārābī and Avicenna (d. 1037). Both of these philosophers tie the nature of beauty to the realisation of proper perfection. In al-Fārābī's words in *The Perfect State*, "[b]eauty [*jamāl*] and brilliance and splendour mean in the case of every existent that it is in its most excellent state of existence and that it has attained its ultimate perfection."[14] This is why God, as the most perfect being, is also the most beautiful. The truest form of beauty, we may notice, is again located in the domain of the transcendent. Yet neither al-Fārābī nor Avicenna appears interested in translating this general idea into a statement concerning human ethical perfection. In his "Epistle on Love," notably, Avicenna has little to say about either the beauty of the natural world or the beauty of human character.[15]

The above survey is not intended to imply that Hellenistic texts were the most important agent in making the application of the concept of beauty to the domain of moral character thinkable for intellectuals in the Islamic world. The connection between ethics and aesthetics seems to have been already enshrined in the semantic scope of the key Arabic terms even before the wide dissemination of Greek philosophy in Islamic culture. The Qurʾan itself provides some interesting testimony in this regard, as it contains a number of passages where the term "beautiful" (*jamīl*) is applied to actions and qualities of character (or to actions as expressive of qualities). It is used to describe patience (Q 12:18, 12:83, 70:5) as also forgiveness (Q 15:85) and the act of releasing women after an early divorce (Q 33:49). Translators approaching these passages have opted for a variety of expressions most of which preserve the aesthetic element, including "handsome," "gracious," "fair," "beautiful," "fitting," "comely," and "sweet."[16] Talk of "beautiful patience" implies that there are different types of patience, some of which are beautiful while others are not. What makes patience beautiful, we learn from Qurʾanic commentators, is for a person to endure hardship uncomplainingly, without resentment and without the need to advertise their suffering to others—in a word, displaying the type of self-command we associate with a noble, magnanimous (Kant might have said: a sublime) spirit.[17]

Whatever the precise developmental route—and it is not my intention to exhaustively plot that here—the association of beauty with the domain of moral character found its way into many of the major lexicographical documents put together by scholars of the Arabic language. The eighteenth-century scholar Murtaḍā al-Zabīdī (d. 1791), for example, defines *jamāl* as *ḥusn* that concerns either physical form (*khalq*) or moral character (*khuluq*) in his celebrated dictionary.[18] The idea also finds expression, albeit in more rudimentary form, in the dictionary of Qurʾanic usage compiled by a scholar who flourished in the same century as al-Ghazālī, and who we know formed one of his main inspirations in matters of ethics, al-Rāghib al-Iṣfahānī. Beauty is of two kinds, self-regarding and other-regarding, the former being a beauty "proper to a person's soul (*nafs*), body, or action."[19]

4 Moral beauty and the paradigm of disinterested love

Some of the preceding discussion has been gritty, revolving as it did around the negotiation of Arabic terms and their meanings. Yet this cannot be avoided if we wish to gain clarity on how the ethical and the aesthetic were brought into relation within important sectors of Islamic culture, and if we wish to build some context for al-Ghazālī's specific account of this relation. Well-versed in the main religious and linguistic sciences of his time but also deeply acquainted with the work of the major philosophers, including al-Fārābī, Avicenna, and Miskawayh, al-Ghazālī stood at the confluence of many of the intellectual streams outlined above. His extensive corpus—al-Ghazālī was a prolific writer of intellectual blockbusters in a range of fields, including law, theology (*kalām*), and polemics, philosophical and otherwise—is watered by these streams in different kinds of ways. In the *Revival of the Religious Sciences*, and to a lesser extent the *Scale of Action*, philosophical ethics and psychology partner up with Sufi thought to create the main framework of al-Ghazālī's virtue-ethical outlook.[1]

These are not, I should underline at the outset, the only works within al-Ghazālī's oeuvre that we may classify under the heading of "ethics." Ethics is also a theme of his theological and legal works, including his treatise on legal theory *The Quintessence of the Principles of Law* and his theological handbook *Moderation in Belief*. In those works, al-Ghazālī's principal interest is in the kind of questions of meta-ethics mentioned earlier. (Are ethical norms known by religious scripture or human reason? Are they objective features or products of divine assignment?) His correlative focus, in adjudicating these questions, is on actions as objects of evaluative assessment (good or bad, obligatory or prohibited). By contrast, in the *Revival of the Religious Sciences* and the *Scale of Action*, his primary concern is with traits of character.[2]

It is in the latter set of works, in which al-Ghazālī unfolds his programme of spiritual and ethical perfection, that we encounter an

DOI: 10.4324/9781003196556-4

ongoing concern with the theme of beauty, and a pervasive enmeshment of the ethical and the aesthetic. It can be observed, on a first level, in al-Ghazālī's main forays into the definition of character. In the *Revival*, he broaches foundational questions of this sort in the book titled *Discipline of the Soul*—one of the most philosophical books of the *Revival*, and the one where al-Ghazālī warms to the theme of character in earnest. A character trait, as he defines it, is "a stable structure (or disposition: *hayʾa*) of the soul which causes actions to issue with facility and ease."[3] This structure represents the "inner form" (*ṣūra bāṭina*) of the soul. The form of a *virtuous* character results when the different powers of the soul are placed in balance. The inner form a person possesses is susceptible to a kind of evaluation directly analogous to the one their outer form invites. "Human beings," al-Ghazālī explains, "are composed of a body that can be perceived by sight (*baṣar*) and a spirit and soul that can be perceived by insight (*baṣīra*). Each of these has a structure and form, whether ugly/bad (*qabīḥ*) or beautiful/lovely (*jamīl*)." A person who is beautiful on the outside is described as having a "fine build" (*ḥasan al-khalq*). A person who is beautiful on the inside is described as having a "fine character" (*ḥasan al-khuluq*).[4]

In framing these points, al-Ghazālī cycles freely between the terms *ḥasan* and *jamīl*. To make the following discussion more navigable without the need to constantly flag the Arabic terms in use, I will temporarily reserve "fine" for *ḥasan* and "beautiful" for *jamīl*. We will need to return to this arrangement for further comment once a few more chess pieces have been put in place.

With virtue—the object of moral concern—placed in an aesthetic framework, it may come as no surprise to find that moral motivation—the desire and pursuit of virtue—is also located in a similar framework. One's aim, al-Ghazālī writes, should be "to adorn one's interior and beautify it through virtue" (*taḥliyyat bāṭinihi wa-tajmīluhu biʾl-faḍīla*).[5] Our aspiration to become virtuous, on an important level, must be an aspiration to become beautiful. As phrased, this point may appear troubling from two separate directions. The normative terms in which it is couched, on the one hand, may evoke perplexity. Surely the desire for beauty is so natural it neither needs no, nor could possibly benefit from, external encouragement, and could hardly constitute an achievement? One way of removing this perplexity might be by taking the point as a way of answering the fundamental question of why be moral (virtuous). "Because it will make you beautiful" (and *this* is something we all want).[6] Yet that leads us to the second difficulty, as it might be queried whether a desire to be beautiful represents an appropriate sort of moral motivation. Put most simply, it is too egoistic and self-referential to fit the part. More deeply, the desire to be beautiful seems to be a desire to *appear* a certain way, rather than to *be* a certain kind of person. This is a way of saying that to acknowledge the aesthetic modality of our perception of *others'* character does not automatically entail that we consider the same modality acceptable when representing the actual or desired state of our *own*.[7]

There are, of course, contexts in which it is perfectly intelligible for us to treat aesthetic responses as objects of normative encouragement. Our aesthetic reactions, after all, often stand in need of education; the experienced art critic, for example, will find things beautiful that the novice will not. Yet in fact al-Ghazālī does not ultimately suppose that our response to *moral* beauty is one of those cases (though there will be nuances to consider).[8] This becomes clear when we turn to another level of his account, where both aspects we have discussed (the nature of virtue and moral motivation) find their deeper foundation. Both of the concerns just outlined also find their answer on this level of al-Ghazālī's account.

Like many of his philosophical (and mutatis mutandis, Sufi) predecessors, al-Ghazālī places God at the heart of his reflections on beauty. It is God who possesses the truest beauty and sublimity; the beauty of all other beings is both inferior to and derivative from it. God's beauty, as among al-Ghazālī's philosophical predecessors, is grounded in his perfection, with all other perfection again standing in a derivative relation to it.[9] The implications of this idea for the ethical life of human beings emerge on at least two levels: how we understand the nature of virtue and how we understand its pursuit. On the one hand, God's character provides nothing less than the criterion for what constitutes virtue (or true virtue).[10] And on the other, and as a corollary, the life of virtue fundamentally is, and should be understood as, a quest to become like God. This idea has a long philosophical lineage, especially among Platonists and Neoplatonists. In the Islamic world, it was given scriptural backing in the form of a well-known hadith that urges believers to "assume the character traits of God" (*takhallaqū bi-akhlāq Allāh*). The idea is explored in the greatest concentration in a short work that al-Ghazālī devotes to an investigation of the names of God, *The Most Exalted Aim in Expounding God's Beautiful Names*. As he makes clear in this work, it is the *aesthetic* response produced by God's attributes—the sense of awe, wonder, and reverence aroused by their grandeur and splendour—that provides the impetus for the ethical striving to acquire them for ourselves. The person who has gained insight into one of the attributes of God is thereby filled with "longing for that attribute, ardour for that grandeur and beauty, and a desire to be adorned by that feature."[11]

The beauty of virtue, thus, ultimately attaches to its divine exemplar. And it is the perception of this beauty that excites our moral aspiration and motivates us to imitate it. To return to the two concerns outlined earlier, this means that, while moral pursuit indeed takes its basis from a desire for beauty, this desire has a different profile from the one that underpins the suspicion of it as a form of moral motivation. This desire is not egocentric and possessive, but allocentric and participatory. It is supported by an understanding that the beauty we strive for properly belongs to another, and even in a derivative sense can only be partially instantiated; and the value of instantiating it is not that we have it, but that we are more connected to another who does, and our relation to whom matters to us. As with the birdsong that exercised al-Ghazālī in the *Revival*, our response to the beauty of virtue is validated not on its own account but through its connection to God. At the same time, what we aspire to in desiring God's beauty are a set of features that represent true perfections. The indissoluble link al-Ghazālī forges between beauty and perfection means that appearance and being—appearing a certain way versus being a certain kind of person—can't quite be cleaved apart.[12]

In the *Exalted Aim*, al-Ghazālī presents admiration and desire for such beauty as responses that come naturally to us. Yet this should not disguise the cognitive achievements such responses involve. Most obviously, we can fail to become aware of God's characteristics, though the implication is that we will naturally experience them as beautiful when we do.[13] On a different level, this model suggests we can be mistaken about the nature of virtue, and hence we may admire perfections that are not really perfections (because not included in God's character), just as we can be mistaken about the reasons why we should pursue virtue (because it is an imitation of God's beautiful character). Against this metaphysical understanding, we are thus likely to need to revise our ordinary ideas about virtue, and consequently our aesthetic responses.

These considerations seem all the more important given that it is our natural reaction to *human* moral beauty that provides us with a starting point for thinking about the reaction merited by God's. This is in fact one of the most significant structural features of that discussion of beauty that has justly dominated all accounts of the theme in al-Ghazālī's oeuvre, namely the discussion that takes place in the book of the *Revival* entitled *On Love*. Unlike the *Exalted Aim*, where the focus is on divine beauty, this book places the moral beauty of human beings at the centre of its concerns, or of what we may call its distinctive "ladder" of love. It is there that al-Ghazālī develops most fully his understanding of the nature and importance of beauty, and of the relation between the beautiful and the good.

That such a discussion takes place in a book dedicated to the topic of love is no coincidence. Like the Plato/Socrates/Diotima of the *Symposium* and their many intellectual heirs, al-Ghazālī believes that love is, at least in part, love of beauty, and that it is as beautiful that God partly commands our passionate love. Yet love, in al-Ghazālī's view, is more complex, and requires sorting. A large part of the book is accordingly spent building a careful taxonomy of the different forms of love. This taxonomy is prefaced by a more programmatic meditation on the concept of love.

Love, as al-Ghazālī defines it, is inseparably connected to a conception of nature and natural function. The things perceived by living beings divide into those that agree with their nature (*ṭabʿ*) and those that do not. "Everything whose perception produces pleasure and delight is beloved to the perceiver … what it means for [an object] to be loved is that one's nature inclines to it (*fi ʾl- ṭabʿ mayl ilayhi*)." Thus, "love signifies the natural inclination toward an object that produces pleasure." Yet as living beings we possess a number of different senses and perceptual powers. Each of these has its own separate nature and to each corresponds a different inclination and form of pleasure, and hence love. Our visual sense, thus, takes pleasure in sight and more specifically in the apprehension of beautiful forms, our sense of hearing in melodies with rhythmic balance, our olfactory sense in pleasant smells. When our nature is sound (*ʿinda al-ṭabʿ al-salīm*), there is thus a definite range of objects in which each of our senses finds satisfaction.[14]

These physical senses, al-Ghazālī goes on to argue, do not exhaust our nature. What makes us human is a sixth sense we possess, which is what people refer to as "reason" or (in a more Sufi idiom) the "heart,"[15] and which contrasts to outer sight as inner insight (*baṣīra bāṭina*). This, too, has its proper range of objects, and the corresponding pleasure it derives upon their attainment. That pleasure far exceeds the one derived through the other senses—at least when our nature is in a sound state. As with the other senses, al-Ghazālī's frames this point using strongly aesthetic terms. "The beauty of those elements perceived through reason surpasses the beauty of the forms available to sight."[16] It is through this sense, al-Ghazālī will say here and elsewhere in the *Revival*, that we perceive God, who forms its most proper object, and the one whose attainment affords us the greatest possible satisfaction.

The ensuing discussion in *On Love* can on one level be taken as a way of answering the following question: What do we love when we love God? This is what I read as the underlying purpose of al-Ghazālī's attempt to sort through the different varieties of love. Love, in al-Ghazālī's view, is individuated by its causes and objects. The most important forms of love are then named as follows:[17]

1 Love of self (*nafs, dhāt*)
2 Love of beneficence (*iḥsān*)
3 Love of an object for its own sake (*li-dhātihi*)
4 Love caused by a hidden affinity (*munāsaba khafiyya*)

Some of these categories speak for themselves. Love of self will seem self-evident. This type of love, al-Ghazālī explains, manifests itself in our concern to perpetuate our existence, but also to perfect our existence. Many of the other objects to which we are habitually attached—our physical integrity and well-being, our material possessions, but also our children, kinsmen, and friends—are loved precisely under their description as conducive to preserving or perfecting our existence.[18] Love of beneficence may also seem self-explanatory: we all love people who act beneficently towards us. This is the description, al-Ghazālī explains, under which we love teachers and doctors, for example. Yet we also love people who act beneficently towards *others*. In one version of his taxonomy, al-Ghazālī distinguishes these as two different causes of love, which I will label beneficence 1 (directed to self) and beneficence 2 (directed to others) for ease of reference. About type 4, I will have little to say. To type 3, I will return in a moment, as it is the one that concerns us most.

Even on this synoptic view, al-Ghazālī's taxonomy may strike us as creaky. Why, for example, make beneficence 1 a separate category, instead of filing it under "love of self"?[19] Yet putting such issues to the side, let us instead attend to the general character of this taxonomy. The taxonomy is meant to be empirical: it intends to represent the facts of human experience. The different forms of love describe the different reasons (and with an eye to 4, the causes) on account of which we actually love. The taxonomy can then be read as accomplishing two things. First, it provides the basis for claiming that God is the most appropriate object of love across its entire spectrum of familiar forms and reasons. If we love our own existence, its perpetuation and its perfection, God is the being that truly merits our love, as it is he who secures these goods. If we love benefactors (whether to self or others), God is the true benefactor, who causally determines, no less, the beneficence of human agents.[20]

Yet the taxonomy has a second drift. Because from an evaluative perspective, these forms are not all equal; some of them are better than others. I take it to be evident that for al-Ghazālī, the best sort of love is intrinsic love.[21] A second aim of the taxonomy is thus to stake the claim that this superior form of love—and hence superior way of loving God—represents a real human possibility.

So what is the nature of that love, and under what description do we empirically meet it? It is the kind of love, al-Ghazālī explains, that we experience when we love something for its own sake or being (*li-dhātihi*), "and not for any gain (*ḥaẓẓ*) we stand to make beyond it; rather, its being is itself the gain (*dhātuhu ʿaynu ḥaẓẓihi*)."[22] It will be appealing, based on this remark, to describe this form of love as "disinterested." Yet as this statement already shows, that would be misleading if taken to imply that we gain nothing whatsoever from the experience. In modern philosophy, the distinction between "interested" and "disinterested" sometimes comes up in the context of characterising the distinctively moral point of view, where it is tied to a contrast between egoistic and non-egoistic motivation. In this capacity, it is sometimes leveraged to question whether ancient philosophers had a concept of morality, though in the reverse direction, the ancient philosophers' lack of this distinction (most fundamentally in conceptualising the virtuous life as the happy one) has also been leveraged to criticise the modern conception of morality.[23] The distinction between interested and disinterested viewpoints is also commonly mobilised in another context, in characterising the nature of aesthetic experience.

The issue is ultimately definitional: it depends on how we define "interest." For his part, al-Ghazālī clearly intends to mark a distinction between the kind of concern that shapes the egoistic standpoint of category 1 and the kind that shapes the standpoint of the present category, with the latter represented as the superior of the two. Yet it is also clear that he believes we have an important stake in the experience he now turns to describe. The experience of intrinsic love affords us a powerful satisfaction in which our nature finds profound fulfilment. Each standpoint can in fact be seen as representing different aspects of our nature, each of which has its corresponding concept of "interest" and sphere of satisfaction. And it is precisely aesthetic experience that al-Ghazālī calls upon to supply his paradigm case of intrinsic love as we humanly know it.

The human love of beauty (*al-jamāl wa'l-ḥusn*) is the clearest example of "disinterested" (in this qualified sense) or intrinsic love. We love beautiful forms for their own sake, and not because of some instrumental purpose they might conceivably serve. Al-Ghazālī's first frame of reference in approaching this point is the way we typically respond to the beauty of the natural world. It is a mistake to think, he writes, that "the only reason we love beautiful forms (*ṣuwar jamīla*) is on account of some [carnal] appetite we want to satisfy." We know from experience that

> people love vegetation and flowing water not because they want to drink the water or eat the vegetation or satisfy some need (*ḥaẓẓ*), but only on account of the visual perception itself (*ruʾya*) … it is the necessary expression of a sound nature (*al-ṭibāʿ al-salīma qāḍiya bi-*) to take pleasure in the contemplation of lights, flowers, or well-formed birds with fine-coloured plumage … indeed, one's cares and sorrows are dispelled as one contemplates them, for no other stake beyond mere contemplation.[24]

The intrinsic love of beautiful forms is here identified with the pleasure taken in the act of visual contemplation and contrasted with an instrumental type of desire towards these objects that might derive from our appetitive nature. This aesthetic response is claimed as a familiar empirical fact about human beings. Love of beauty is something we are naturally disposed to (*al-jamāl maḥbūb biʾl-ṭabʿ*).[25]

From a philosophical perspective, al-Ghazālī's account will seem especially interesting in evoking open comparison with modern analyses of aesthetic experience. Although, as I have suggested, his understanding of its "disinterested" character has to be approached carefully, the contrast that underpins his account places it in clear conversation with a prominent philosophical view of this character that is often associated with Kant. The hallmark of aesthetic judgements, on this view, is that they do not implicate (presuppose or stimulate) desire for their object. As Roger Scruton puts it, aesthetic experience involves enjoyment of an object for its own sake, which means having a "desire to go on hearing, looking at, or in some other way having experience of *X*, where there is no reason for this desire in terms of any other desire or appetite that the experience of *X* may fulfil."[26] Al-Ghazālī's emphasis on the therapeutic or palliative effect of aesthetic experience, and the experience of nature in particular, forges equally suggestive connections. Among philosophers, a similar view has been paradigmatically expressed by Schopenhauer. For Schopenhauer, the contemplation of nature enables us to transcend the will-full perspective of individual subjectivity and provides us with a temporary reprieve from suffering. "This is why the man tormented by passions, want, or care, is so suddenly revived, cheered, and comforted by a single, free glance into nature."[27]

Yet it is al-Ghazālī's next move, and the next frame of reference he introduces to conceptualise the human love of beauty, that forms the flagship of his account. And here, his view and that of most modern philosophers of aesthetics part ways. Contemporary aestheticians, as mentioned earlier, typically focus on nature and art as the paradigm objects of aesthetic attention. This focus goes hand in hand with an emphasis on availability to sensory perception as a criterion for aesthetic properties. In the view of one prominent exponent, Nick Zangwill, sensory properties such as colours and sounds are necessary for aesthetic properties (though they might not be sufficient), so that "without sensory properties, there would be no aesthetic properties." Hence, any application of aesthetic terms to objects not perceived by the five senses must be metaphorical.[28]

More recently, this type of view has come in for sharp critique from other philosophical quarters.[29] It is precisely this narrow view that al-Ghazālī himself brings up in the next stage of his discussion and offers to interrogate and refine. This is a view he takes to typify how the ordinary man on the street thinks about beauty. Ordinary people tend to assume that only concrete physical things, typically things we can *see* which have shape and colour and size, more typically still human beings, can be beautiful. This understanding is too narrow on two counts: in sidelining the forms of beauty registered by other physical senses and in overlooking the forms of beauty that are not registered by a physical sense at all. And here, it is the case of moral beauty—of a beauty attaching to human character—that constitutes al-Ghazālī's central exemplar.

To correct and enlarge the popular conception of the beautiful, al-Ghazālī begins by appealing to the data of ordinary language using a progressively wider palette of examples. We speak not only of a fine-looking person but also of a "fine horse," a "fine writing hand" (*khaṭṭ ḥasan*), and a "fine sound" or voice (*ṣawt ḥasan*). More importantly, we also speak of "fine character" (*khuluq ḥasan*), of a "fine course of conduct" (*sīra ḥasana*),[30] and of "beautiful character traits" (*akhlāq jamīla*), such as temperance, courage, piety, and generosity.[31] These beautiful qualities, which constitute the inner form of a person, are not perceived through the senses, but through inner insight (*al-baṣīra al-bāṭina*).

Thus, even though ordinary people, when prompted to pronounce on the topic of beauty, would be likely to give a restrictive account of its objects, a more inclusive conception is implicit in their own patterns of linguistic usage. In the *Exalted Aim*, al-Ghazālī suggests these two applications—to sensory and to non-sensory objects—represent different stages of the development of language, identifying the former as historically prior. "The term 'beautiful' was originally (*fi'l-aṣl*) appointed to signify the outward form perceivable through sight ... and was later transferred to the inward form perceivable through insight."[32] Yet even if historically posterior, the latter is now enshrined in ordinary linguistic usage.

In order for this more inclusive conception of the beautiful to become reflectively available, the average person needs to consult not only their linguistic habits but also their patterns of emotional response—specifically how they respond to the kinds of virtuous qualities outlined above. "The person characterised by them naturally arouses love (*maḥbūb biʾl-ṭabʿ*) in all those who become cognisant of his features." Witness the love we experience towards religious exemplars, such as the prophet Muḥammad, his companions, and the founders of the schools of law. Our love cannot attach to the physical form of these figures—that agglomerate of "bones, flesh, and skin"—as this has long turned to dust. It attaches rather to the inner form constituted by these praiseworthy characteristics. It is these characteristics that ground a person's identity, making it the case that "Abū Bakr al-Ṣiddīq was Abū Bakr al-Ṣiddīq,"[33] and the form they constitute endures through time.[34]

The moral and intellectual virtues such figures possess thus spell out a non-physical form of beauty that we register when we respond with love. This emotional response—to complete al-Ghazālī's thought and draw certain ideas together—tracks a relation of natural fitness that looks in two directions. On the one hand, these virtues constitute the proper perfection of their possessors' nature as human beings. Like many of his philosophical predecessors, al-Ghazālī refers the concept of beauty to the concept of perfection. An entity is beautiful when "it realises the perfection appropriate to and possible for it." In the fuller expression of the *Exalted Aim*, "when the inner form is perfect, harmoniously constituted, and unites all perfections appropriate to it, as it ought and in the manner it ought, it is beautiful in relation to the insight that perceives it"—suited to the observer in a way that produces in him a sense of joy and delight.[35] Beauty, as this remark flags, is always relative to a perceiver. And taken as an object of perception, the perfection of others' nature also represents the natural fulfilment of the *observers'* special cognitive power as human beings.

One important point this also brings out is that the emotional response at issue is no brute passion, as a long-standing tradition with both modern and pre-modern supporters would have it, representing emotions as blind pushes and pulls fundamentally opposed to reason. Emotions, here, respond to reasons; our love of these exemplars is based on a judgement about their moral features and is *justified* on that basis. In another book of the *Revival*, al-Ghazālī brings up the relation between cognitions or beliefs (*maʿārif*), states (*aḥwāl*), and actions (*aʿmāl*), and explains that actions result from states, and states from cognitions. "States," in al-Ghazālī's adaptation of this Sufi term, typically refers to emotions.[36] This cognitivist view of emotions is reflected in his present discussion.

Returning to al-Ghazālī's previous statement about long-dead figures, his point can be taken as an attempt to address a puzzle that inevitably comes up once we accept that we can experience emotional reactions towards beings that lack physical realisation in the natural world. When we love a person who lacks physical embodiment for their moral character, what exactly is it we love? This is a puzzle that comes up equally whether we're considering deceased historical characters or imaginary characters, such as those we meet in fictional works, notwithstanding the differences between the two cases. With regard to the latter, many philosophers of art would recognise this as the special problem sometimes labelled the "paradox of fiction."[37] One option would be to say that what we love is simply the mental representation we have of that character, regardless of whether there is an actually existing entity that this is a representation *of*. Al-Ghazālī, as I read his account, does not want to take that option (in this respect, he appears uninterested in the emotional responses we might have to purely fictional characters). Instead, he seems to want to insist that the object of our love has actual existence external to our mind, and that its existence is temporally enduring.

This begs two obvious questions. In what sense do the non-physical (moral) features in question endure? And just how do we have epistemic access to the non-physical (moral) form they spell out? Of these questions, it is the latter that receives the clearest answer in al-Ghazālī's discussion, one that locates his account firmly within the literary practices of his religious community while also forging links to a wider context. For a religious believer, access to the religious exemplars of the historical past is provided by narratives, oral and written. We may think of the hadith reports detailing the Prophet's conduct and of the variety of genres recording the biographies of eminent individuals in the Islamic world, such as biographical dictionaries and works belonging to the genre of laudatory (*manāqib*) literature. The Prophet in particular was the focus of a specific literary genre, the *shamāʾil* (literally "characteristics"), which built on hadith reports to offer a concentrated account of the Prophet's perfections that both reflected and was designed to evoke attitudes of admiration and love.[38] For a counterpart outside the Islamic world, we only need to think of Plutarch's *Lives*. It is such narratives (*siyar*), al-Ghazālī indicates, that provide epistemic access to the moral character of historical individuals.

In certain parts of his discussion, al-Ghazālī encourages us to think that this way of answering the question about epistemic access to moral features translates into the following answer to the metaphysical question about their mode of realisation and temporal endurance: the beauteous form of these individuals exists *in* these narratives (*al-jamāl mawjūd fi'l-siyar*).[39] Yet closer investigation suggests that, for al-Ghazālī, this explanation is incomplete. Taken alone, this explanation would allow for the possibility that the object of our love should be a mere mental construct with no mind-independent correlate. Al-Ghazālī distances himself from this possibility by making a couple of related links. On one level, he stakes the claim that there is a causal relation between the virtuous character of these individuals and the narratives that represent this character. Such "praiseworthy features … are the sources of beautiful accounts [of their lives]" (*al-ṣifāt al-maḥmūda…hiya maṣādir al-siyar al-jamīla*). Yet this relation is not merely historical. The implication is that, unlike the physical form which perishes, these features still endure, and that the statements found in different narratives are true because the object to which they refer still exists. It is this existing object to which our own emotional response attaches when we hear or see it described and we react with love. "The thing loved is the source of the accounts, that is to say, the praiseworthy character traits and noble virtues."[40]

The above is an attempt to reconstruct al-Ghazālī's understanding on the basis of evidence that is not always explicit and unambiguous. Al-Ghazālī's interest in this context is not in teasing out these metaphysical and epistemological implications. As reconstructed, his view would seem to presuppose some version of the immaterial survival of the soul, in which these kinds of features would inhere. It leaves open a number of puzzles, including how we might understand the endurance of moral features that, on al-Ghazālī's view, only make sense relative to the need to govern the physical body.[41] Also less than fully developed is al-Ghazālī's understanding of the exact modality through which verbal and literary representations can evoke an emotional response to moral virtue. This seems all the more remarkable given the deep conviction reflected in his discussion concerning the power of narratives to induce such response.

> When we wish to arouse love toward any given person, be they absent or present, living or dead, in a young boy with his natural inclinations intact, our only option is to go to great lengths in describing their courage, generosity, learning, and other praiseworthy characteristics.[42] Once he has acquired a belief to that effect, he can't resist: he can't help but love them.[43]

This, to reiterate, is how we conceive a sense of love towards the religious and other historical personalities named earlier (and how we acquire *reasons* for our affective response to them). Describe the pre-Islamic Arab icon Ḥātim al-Ṭāʾī as generous, the early Muslim military commander Khālid ibn al-Walīd as brave, and "our hearts are *necessarily* drawn to them in love" (*aḥabbathum al-qulūb ḥubban ḍarūriyyan*). Indeed, al-Ghazālī next widens his scope,

> if it is reported that a certain king living in some distant part is conducting himself with justice and beneficence (*al-ʿadl waʾl-iḥsān*) and spreading good everywhere around him, people are overcome with a sense of love for him. This is the case even though the people who feel such love have no reason to hope they might be [personally] touched by his beneficence, given the … great distance that separates them. Thus, human beings are not capable of only loving those who benefit them; rather benefactors are loved for themselves (*maḥbūb fī nafsihi*), even if their beneficence never reaches the person who loves them. For all beauty and fineness (*jamāl wa-ḥusn*) is an object of love; forms divide into outer and inner, and "beauty" and "fineness" apply to both.[44]

Al-Ghazālī's account of the efficacy of narratives in evoking emotional response invites a number of questions. Do all kinds of descriptions of character evoke love, or only a subset with specific features? Does the description of beautiful character need to satisfy certain aesthetic criteria—to be beautiful itself? This hands over to questions about literary aesthetics that were by no means marginal to Islamic culture, not least given the cultural primacy of the Qurʾan and the multilevel intellectual preoccupation with its credentials as a literary document of unparalleled beauty. Such questions had also been enlivened by Greek philosophical reflection on related topics, where, as Taneli Kukkonen notes, engagement with Aristotle's *Rhetoric* and *Poetics* ensured "that a sizeable body of work formed around the question of what constitutes pleasing, effective, and persuasive speech."[45] Here, al-Ghazālī does not seem interested in such literary questions.

Bracketing such questions therefore, it is worth making a couple of observations about this long quotation. One observation may seem dry and formalistic, but it has a bearing on a later stage of our discussion so it is worth recording. In this passage, al-Ghazālī clearly fuses what had appeared as separate items in his earlier taxonomy: love of beneficence (specifically, disinterested beneficence 2) and love of (moral) beauty. A second observation has wider reach. It may be noted that virtually all of the exemplars of beautiful character that al-Ghazālī picks to illustrate his thesis share one fundamental feature: distance from the observer, whether in time (the prophet Muḥammad, his companions, etc.) or space (the king). This, as the above passage itself suggests, is a deliberate design, as it serves al-Ghazālī's purpose of arguing that the response to moral beauty does not stem from any bearing the relevant qualities might have on our self-interest narrowly conceived. Whether this is fully convincing is a question I will be returning to, but for the moment I will note that one result of this framing is a remarkable neglect of our emotional reactions to and loving relationships with living people, notably friends.[46] This in turn has another interesting result, which is important for the philosophical development of al-Ghazālī's core idea.

Put simply, the effect of the focus on absentee exemplars of virtue is to enforce a particularly strong separation between the inner and the outer, or the intelligible and the sensory, and to ensure that moral beauty is conceptualised in the greatest possible abstraction from any physical manifestations the latter might have. That, however, overlooks the significance of such manifestations in the way character enters our everyday experience. While the character of spatiotemporally distant exemplars—such as Socrates, the Buddha, or Jesus Christ, to name some celebrated instances outside the Islamic tradition—typically becomes available to us through verbal narratives and representations, living human beings reveal their character to us in a more complex set of ways. This will often involve extended observation of an individual's patterns of acting and choosing, and of their expressed thoughts and feelings. It will be several occasions of seeing a person redden with anger at a perceived slight, or seeing a person's eyes grow moist while someone unburdens their griefs to them, that eventually lead us to describe the one as "irascible" or "proud" and the other as "tender-hearted" or "compassionate." While a single expressed thought, expressed feeling, or observed action will rarely suffice as a basis for attributing a certain type of character to a person, it will form part of this basis; and once a judgement of character has been formed, a single action, thought, or feeling will often be perceived as its immediate manifestation. This is partly illustrated by the incident from *Jane Eyre* referenced earlier, where the heroine, against a background of extended interactions with her good friend Helen Burns that have given her an understanding of her overall character, finds herself gazing on her wonderingly one evening and remarking on the "beauty ... of meaning, of movement, of radiance" she perceives in her face. This type of expressive behaviour, crucially, provides character with its physical anchor and embodiment. The simple insight that, in living human beings, character can in an important sense be *seen* is captured in Wittgenstein's lapidary formulation that "the human body is the best picture of the human soul."[47] The related insight that our character can achieve a lasting expression in our body—that the picture of the soul may be *permanently* painted—finds its most spectacular fictional representation in Oscar Wilde's *The Picture of Dorian Gray*.[48]

The manifestation of character in the human body seems to me a point that has a potentially important role to play in supporting the philosophical plausibility of the concept of moral beauty. While it has not been a central focus in all recent defences of the idea, it has been a theme in at least some. Ian Kidd, for example, builds his account of moral beauty on the fact that the inner virtues of exemplary individuals achieve expression in "outer bodily comportment available for perceptual experience," which allows us to "*see* tranquillity in their face, *hear* calm in their voice and *sense* equanimity in their demeanour" and to experience these expressions as beautiful. Talk of "inner" virtues and "inner" beauty, thus, "should not be taken to imply any radical separation of the inner and outer aspects of a person."[49]

Now what is interesting is that al-Ghazālī himself elsewhere gives ample recognition to this point and to the relations of mutual reciprocity that hold between body and soul more generally. In one place of the *Scale* where he is discussing the concept of outer or bodily beauty, he makes the surprising statement that such "beauty usually reveals the virtuousness of the soul."[50] The claim that virtue and physical beauty are inseparably linked had important precedents in the classical world. It was the centrality of this idea that Nietzsche had in mind in the *Twilight of the Idols* when he stated that "ugliness … is among the Greeks almost a refutation."[51] The idea also found its way into the Islamic tradition through a variety of channels, including Greek wisdom literature. In one development of this idea, it is a question of the concomitance of two independent qualities—the physically beautiful person is *also* typically virtuous—explicable through a common cause: a balanced humoural mixture.[52] But al-Ghazālī's continuation in fact shows that what he has in mind is the rather more basic insight picked out above. Thus, "the eyes and the face are a mirror that reflects one's interior, which is why anger and evilness make themselves manifest in them." "When the light of the soul becomes radiant, it communicates itself to the body"—precisely as Helen Burns' had done in Charlotte Brontë's account.[53] The body expresses the soul. The beauty of the soul thus typically has a sensory correlate; in a very real sense, this beauty can be seen. On al-Ghazālī's terms, it would seem more accurate to say that what we find beautiful, confronted with living human beings, is the soul as available to a *combination* of sight and insight.

There are thus interesting insights about the relationship between inner and outer beauty to be mined from other parts of al-Ghazālī's oeuvre—insights that, fleshed out further, might help provide a different kind of philosophical credence to the concept of moral beauty. But these insights are not integrated into his most concentrated discussion of the theme, in the book *On Love*, which works with a more rigid distinction between outer and inner. This evidently reflects the purposes of this discussion. Its ultimate concern is not the beauty of flesh-and-blood human beings—in whom body and soul stand in intimate relations—but the beauty of God, and its focus is not the relationship between humans but the human relationship to God. The discussion we have followed provides the basis for the claim that critically interests al-Ghazālī: In God, the virtues that we love in human beings are united and realised in their truest and most perfect form. God is thus the most deserving object of a love responsive to beauty.

One way of understanding al-Ghazālī's discussion, as I suggested earlier, is as an attempt to establish that this superior form of love is possible for human beings. This accounts for the empirical emphasis of his discussion, which presents itself as a series of claims about how human beings actually respond to certain kinds of objects and considerations. How convincing are these claims? In particular, is it the case that ordinary people respond to moral excellence in the ways al-Ghazālī describes?

Both philosophers and psychologists have had much to say about the ways in which people respond to the perceived moral excellence of others. Ranging from the Platonic views we already touched upon, to Aristotle's remarks about "emulation" (*zelos*) as the emotion felt paradigmatically by the young that fuels their aspiration to acquire goods they recognise in others, to Jonathan Haidt and fellow-psychologists' focus on "elevation" as a response to moral excellence or Kristján Kristjánsson's "moral awe," there has been no shortage of commentary on the nature of these responses. More recently, Panos Paris has mined a number of empirical studies to argue for the more specific claim (closer to al-Ghazālī's) that moral virtues are experienced by people as "beautiful" and moral vices as "ugly."[54]

None of these studies incorporate the empirical claim that these types of emotional response are universal and exceptionless. Is this an assumption that al-Ghazālī makes, and that he requires for his argument? Do all people respond to moral beauty in the way he describes, and is it problematic if they don't? The answer to this question in fact points to an important qualification in the way we understand the character of his claim. In several of the statements quoted earlier, al-Ghazālī described this emotional response as a "natural" one. Taking pleasure in natural beauty is "the necessary expression of a sound nature" (*al-ṭibāʿ al-salīma qāḍiya bi-*); a "young boy with his natural inclinations intact" will respond with love to descriptions of beautiful character. Yet these expressions clearly signal the possibility that such a response may fail. To say that it is a natural response is not to say that it is actually universal. Our true nature can in fact be prevented from achieving expression; it can be corrupted. As among ancient philosophers, and among other figures in the Islamic milieu theorising the key concept of the human constitution (*fiṭra*), al-Ghazālī's concept of human nature is normative.[55] *Healthy* human beings will respond this way. This does not make empirical facts irrelevant: if such a response were the exception rather than the rule, it would create a challenge for a normative view. The fact that al-Ghazālī does not confront that challenge in the *Revival* can be taken as a sign that he safely assumed most of his readers would recognise his account of themselves as true.[56]

This point links to another question. Because one way we might understand what it means for our response to moral excellence to fail is that we might fail to respond to what is *truly* excellent, and instead admire qualities that are not genuine perfections or admire individuals who are not truly worthy of admiration. Admiring the wrong qualities or the wrong people in fact seems like a more realistic danger than (the almost inhuman) possibility that we might admire nobody or nothing at all. As mentioned earlier, al-Ghazālī holds at least one theoretical view that would open up the possibility that our pre-reflective judgements of (and emotional responses to) character might be mistaken and require revision. God is the measure of virtue; hence a character trait is only a virtue if it is a virtue in God. In other contexts, he also articulates an instrumental view of moral virtue in particular, which implies that a character trait is a moral virtue if it is instrumental to the realisation of our intellectual potentialities.[57] To the extent that these high-level views affect the qualities we identify as true virtues, and to the extent that ordinary people can be ignorant of these views, it would seem that our natural judgements of character are not infallible and would need some kind of education. In this context, all that can be said is that al-Ghazālī does not flag this need. We may speculate that this reflects a judgement that his argument simply did not require it.

5 A conflict in al-Ghazālī's ethics?

My aim in the preceding discussion has not been to provide an exhaustive analysis of al-Ghazālī's account, and there are several aspects—including ones integral to his culminating theological claim—that I will have to leave untouched. Al-Ghazālī's transition from our response to the moral beauty of human beings to the moral beauty of God does not, to briefly name one issue, seem to me entirely seamless, and to preserve as much of the phenomena as it would need to effortlessly succeed.[1]

These are questions for another day. In the above, I have tried to work through the main contours of al-Ghazālī's account of the relation between the good and the beautiful and to probe some of its philosophical interest, in the hope of making it available to those united by a belief that the notion of moral beauty merits recovery and re-articulation. Al-Ghazālī's bid to expand the narrow concept of beauty as applying solely to sensory objects, and his suggestion that we view moral character as an intelligible form susceptible of aesthetic response, will resonate strongly with some of the most recent philosophical initiatives in that direction.[2]

From a historical perspective, it is of course al-Ghazālī's links to earlier expressions of similar ideas that will stand out. The distinction between sensory and intelligible beauty, as already mentioned, was a staple of Neoplatonic thinking, as was the understanding of natural and artistic beauty as a manifestation of divine beauty. This distinction found direct expression in the adapted Arabic translation of Plotinus' *Enneads* (the *Theology of Aristotle*). There, too, we meet the idea of moral character as a key exemplar of intelligible beauty. The emphasis on moral beauty also registers in Galen's *Peri Ethon*, joined, significantly, to an open affirmation of the love that human beings naturally experience towards it, which may lead them to prefer the fine even where it conflicts with their immediate advantage.[3] The

DOI: 10.4324/9781003196556-5

close conjunction of the good and the beautiful attested in these and other philosophical texts also finds expression in the more popular genre of Greek wisdom literature, which left a wide intellectual trace in Islamic culture.[4] From such sources, these ideas found their way into prominent philosophical works written in Arabic, including those by al-Fārābī, Avicenna, and the Ikhwān al-Ṣafāʾ.

The precise balance of influences at work in al-Ghazālī's articulation of his ideas has been debated. Certain commentators have argued that the idea of God's beauty in particular was fundamentally alien to Semitic culture and could only be regarded as a graft from the Hellenistic philosophical tradition.[5] Yet the connection between the good and the beautiful, as we have seen, was inscribed in the very data of the Arabic language, into which such intellectual grafts were received. This is a point highlighted by Franz Rosenthal when commenting on the "responsive chord" that the equation of beauty with the ethical and spiritual good in Greek wisdom literature struck in Semitic monotheism.[6] This same connection, as we also saw earlier, is reflected in a number of important linguistic documents that represent both standards of linguistic usage (notably the Qurʾan) and also systematic attempts to describe the principles of that usage, such as the various types of dictionaries compiled by Arab lexicographers. The latter type of source, to be sure, is not itself immune to questions about the influence of Hellenistic philosophical ideas. In his lexicon of Qurʾanic usage, for example, al-Rāghib—an important source for al-Ghazālī—ascribes beauty to the soul and also distinguishes between a form of the "fine" (*ḥasan*) that is accessible by sight (*baṣar*) and a form that is accessible by insight (*baṣīra*).[7] Yet al-Rāghib is known to have been receptive to philosophical influence and is commonly described as the first major intellectual who tried to wed philosophical ideas about ethics into a scriptural framework.[8]

There are thus various complexities involved in trying to disentangle the genealogy of the ideas we have been considering in al-Ghazālī's work. Here, my aim is not to have the final word on such issues, a task I leave to more competent scholars. Having worked through the main outline of al-Ghazālī's account of moral beauty in the *Revival*—with a few satellite texts roped in as needed—I want to raise a question about its place within al-Ghazālī's oeuvre as a whole. This question, as we shall see, will invite us to give closer attention to certain aspects of this account and its way of relating the beautiful and the good.

Al-Ghazālī, as mentioned earlier, was the author of a large number of works belonging to different kinds of genres. The more specific subset of his output that we would be happy to slide under the heading of "ethics" is itself cut from different types of cloth. While we might hesitate to describe al-Ghazālī's works of theology and legal theory—notably *Moderation in Belief* and the *Quintessence of the Principles of Law*—as works of ethics taken as a whole,[9] they treat topics that represent recognisable ethical concerns. This includes above all the cluster of questions commonly treated under the rubric of "(what makes/makes us judge) right and wrong" (*al-ḥusn wa'l-qubḥ/al-taḥsīn wa'l-taqbīḥ*) or "the qualifications of actions" (*aḥkām al-af'āl*), where characteristic meta-ethical questions were raised about the ontology and epistemology of value.

There, al-Ghazālī had defended an Ash'arite view of these issues, which made scripture foundational on two interrelated levels: ethical norms depend ontologically on scripture, and human beings depend epistemically on scripture to access these norms. "Good (*ḥasan*)," on this view, is "whatever the religious Law declared to be good by assigning praise to its agent."[10] While al-Ghazālī recognised that "good" and "bad" were not terms of art introduced by scripture and that they have led and continue to lead an ordinary life in the way people think and talk outside scripture, he took this naturalistic usage to be irrelevant from a normative point of view. In its ordinary usage, "good" is whatever agrees with a person's purposes; and what's good in my view will be bad in yours if our purposes conflict. Variable, relative, and subjective, this sense of "good" and "bad" has no normative importance. It certainly does not pick out objective moral qualities of actions, as Mu'tazilite theologians had argued, and it just as certainly does not reflect the moral pronouncements of pure reason, as again the Mu'tazilites had claimed. Behind this usage of "good" are subjective and wayward human wants.

There was an important nuance in this view. Al-Ghazālī recognised that it is our desire for our personal well-being and our fear of coming to harm that gives the religious Law its psychological purchase and power to obligate. We all want what's good for us. Call this an evaluative judgement if you wish—we all *judge* our welfare to be *good*—so long as we're clear that it stems from a natural inclination rather than from a pure exercise of rationality. "We do not deny," al-Ghazālī writes in *Moderation*, that human beings are "incited by their natural disposition (*ṭab'uhu*) to protect themselves from harm … there is nothing objectionable in applying the term 'obligation' to this incitement."[11] In its basic sense, an act is "obligatory" if failure to perform it would lead to harm. When the Law confronts us with its commands and prohibitions, it engages this fundamental natural inclination by informing us that certain actions carry have beneficial consequences while certain others will be followed by harm.[12]

This natural mode of evaluation, it will be noted, is egoistic: what is good and bad is what is good and bad for *me*. The emphasis on egoistic motivation was a signature of al-Ghazālī's and his Ashʿarite predecessors' theology. In the words of the *Quintessence*, "every person is formed by nature to love himself."[13] This emphasis partly came as a response to Muʿtazilite efforts to establish that human beings are motivated by moral considerations and are capable of acting disinterestedly. Ordinary people (so the Muʿtazilites) are known to act in ways that cannot be simply explained by self-interest: they rush to intervene when they see the blind about to come to harm, they help guide those who have lost their way, they cling faithfully to their oaths even at the cost of their lives. They do these kinds of things even when they have no expectation of praise (nobody is looking) and no expectation of a heavenly reward (they believe in no God). The only conceivable reason, hence, is their knowledge that such acts are morally right.

I have set this out at some length because it is essential for explaining why al-Ghazālī's account of moral beauty in the *Revival* should strike us as deeply puzzling. A person studying al-Ghazālī's treatment of ethics in his theological and legal works, and then turning to consider the account of moral beauty in the works we have surveyed, could be forgiven for supposing these works were written by entirely different individuals. In the former set, al-Ghazālī denies that reason gives access to ethical value. Any extra-scriptural evaluative judgements we make are grounded in our nature conceived in appetitive terms. "Nature" (*ṭabʿ*) is a concept that also features centrally in the discussion of the *Revival*. Yet there, it is explicitly framed in *rational* terms. It is our rational nature that we manifest in responding to moral beauty: we perceive it through "inner insight," a cognitive power that al-Ghazālī is happy to identify with reason.[14] "The beauty of those elements perceived through reason (*al-maʿānī al-mudraka biʾl-ʿaql*)," we heard him say before introducing moral beauty, "surpasses the beauty of the forms available to sight." Unlike the naturalistic evaluations considered in al-Ghazālī's theological and legal works (*good* is whatever agrees with *my* purposes), this reaction to the good/beautiful does not vary among individuals, though it may occasionally fail where nature has been perverted from its course: people typically if not unfailingly respond with love to the perceived excellence of others' character. This reaction is also not subjective: although, as noted earlier, al-Ghazālī's overall account implies that it might require a certain degree of education, the emphasis in the *Revival* is that it responds to what is truly beautiful and a genuine perfection in itself. Most astonishing of all, human beings love the good/beautiful for its own sake, and not for any narrow egoistic purposes it may serve. We love the beautiful "not for any gain (*ḥaẓẓ*) we stand to make beyond it; rather, its being is itself the gain." This was the point illustrated, among other things, by al-Ghazālī's example of the king living in a far-flung corner of the earth who is bruited to be a paragon of justice and beneficence. "[P]eople are overcome with a sense of love for him," even though they "have no reason to hope they might be [personally] touched by his beneficence, given the … great distance that separates them."

What makes this last example particularly startling is just how uncannily it echoes the examples that Muʿtazilite theologians appealed to in building their own case for moral rationalism. The basic architecture is identical. Conjure a situation where human beings exhibit morally interesting behaviour (Muʿtazilites: a person sees a blind man in danger and leaps to help; al-Ghazālī: a person hears about a just and beneficent man and responds with love). Construct situation so as to artificially bracket personal gain (Muʿtazilites: the good deed takes place in a remote location that precludes praise; al-Ghazālī: the good man is based in a remote location that precludes benefit). In his theological and legal works, al-Ghazālī had ripped these kinds of arguments to shreds using a variety of strategies. One of these involved querying whether personal gain could ever be isolated as effectively as the Muʿtazilites suggested. We have been habituated from a young age to associate certain kinds of actions with the pleasant experience of praise; this hardwiring will not be undone by the contingent absence of an actual observer.[15]

It is by no means difficult to imagine how this last weapon could be mobilised against al-Ghazālī's own example. Other responses suggest themselves with equal facility. The moral exemplars he focuses on, for instance—prophets and other religious personalities—would be naturally viewed by the average believer as enhancing or as having enhanced their personal good.[16] As for the case of the distant king, one might simply redeploy a point al-Ghazālī himself makes in an earlier book of the *Revival*, *On the Condemnation of Status and Dissimulation*, in the context of defending his claim that human beings seek status and honour (*jāh*) because this gives them power over others and makes others serve their advantage. To the objection that people are known to thirst for fame even in faraway lands where there is no realistic prospect of deriving advantage, al-Ghazālī essentially responds: nothing seems unrealistic to our anxious self-concern. In other words, it may be an irrational hope, but a hope of advantage is still involved.[17]

In his legal and theological works, of course, al-Ghazālī's focus was on actions as evaluative objects. In the *Revival* and affiliated works, by contrast, his focus is on character and the virtues. This is reflected in the cases constructed above: whereas the Muʿtazilites focus on an action (an instance of helping behaviour), al-Ghazālī focuses on the emotional response to a state of character (justice and beneficence). Yet what is the significance of this distinction, and what help could it provide towards resolving the puzzle? It is true that the relation between the action-focused ethical viewpoint of al-Ghazālī's theological and legal works and the virtue-centred viewpoint of the *Revival* and affiliated works requires clarification. In one of the books of the *Revival, On Patience and Gratitude*, al-Ghazālī offers us a limpid account of the relationship between action and character in which he assigns evaluative primacy unequivocally to the latter.[18] This programmatic view is reflected in the discussion of beauty in the book *On Love*, where at one point al-Ghazālī remarks that while the real object of our love is the inner state of character, it is of course through its external effects that this inner state becomes knowable to us—and that is to say, through the actions that express it. We love people like the prophet Muḥammad, his companions, or the founders of the schools of law

> on account of the fineness (*ḥusn*) of what they manifest to us, yet not on account of the fineness of their [outer] form, nor on account of the fineness of their actions. Rather, the fineness of their actions reveals the fineness of the attributes that are the source of the actions.[19]

Virtue is expressed in action; and while we indeed experience virtuous action as fine, our ultimate object of love is the virtuous character it reveals. Taken both as a psychological and an ethical claim, this is a view that unites al-Ghazālī to many philosophical theorists of the virtues, ancient and modern. Hume puts the point relevantly in his *Treatise*:

> [W]hen we praise any actions, we regard only the motives that produced them, and consider the actions as signs or indications of certain principles in the mind and temper. The external performance has no merit. We must look within to find the moral quality. This we cannot do directly; and therefore fix our attention on actions, as on external signs.[20]

Now this account of the relationship between the value of action and character *as presented in the Revival* is not the same as an explanation of the relationship between the viewpoints of the two sets of works, action-focused and virtue-focused. Yet if we take our bearings from this account, it will be hard to see how the differential focus of each set could explain the overall differences in their viewpoints on ethical value, and why positions that al-Ghazālī adopted vis-à-vis one evaluative object (action) should cease to apply vis-à-vis another (virtue). As the last quotation suggests, action may not be the ultimate resting place of our judgement "fine," but our judgement rests on it nevertheless; and although its value may be relative, it crucially presupposes a judgement about what has non-derivative intrinsic value.[21] This is a view to which it is difficult to imagine the al-Ghazālī of the *Moderation* assenting.

Coming from the *Revival*, it is in fact easy to envisage how many of the standard Muʿtazilite examples of morally interesting behaviour might in principle be re-described using virtue terms. Keeping an oath at pain of death: an instance of *fidelity and courage*. Saving the drowning and helping the blind: an instance of *kindness and benevolence*. This is a redescription that the al-Ghazālī of the *Revival* would wholeheartedly approve of. Yet what is interesting is that the possibility of such a move is signalled by the *Quintessence* itself, for all its monocular focus on action as an object of evaluation. Reporting on the Muʿtazilites, he states their claim that all intelligent beings judge it good to "show fortitude before the sword" (*al-ṣabr ʿala'l-sayf*) rather than betray one's faith; nobody would deny that the noble traits of character (*makārim al-akhlāq*) are fine things.[22]

These and other considerations make it impossible to keep the accounts of the two sets of works apart and to prevent them from entering into relations; and once brought together, they would appear to be in open conflict. What makes al-Ghazālī's position in the *Revival* doubly remarkable, viewed against the history of theological debates about ethics, is the following observation. In these debates, the aesthetic application of the term "fine" or "good" (*ḥasan*) had been weaponised by Ashʿarites *against the Muʿtazilite position*. Al-Ghazālī himself provides an exemplary specimen of this pattern of argument in both the *Moderation* and the *Quintessence*. Judgements of "moral" approval regarding actions are not objective, reason-based, and universal—they are as relative, temperament-based, and idiosyncratic as judgements of "aesthetic" approval. One person finds x beautiful, another does not. Wasn't that exactly what al-Ghazālī said about our moral responses? One person finds x good, another does not. The following remark from the *Quintessence* brings the argument into full view:

> the application of the term "good" (*ḥasan*) and "bad" to actions … resembles its application to [physical] forms. If a person's nature (*ṭabʿ*) is attracted to the form or sound of a certain individual he declares them "fine" (*ḥasan*), whereas if his nature is

repelled by an individual he declares them "ugly". Many people are experienced as repulsive by one nature and as attractive by another, so they will be "fine-looking" as far as the one is concerned and "ugly" for the other.[23]

In the *Revival*, the appeal to "nature" serves to make a claim about the universality of aesthetic reactions. "Nature" means "human nature." Here, by contrast, it refers to individual nature, to what is peculiar to each person rather than shared by all. Aesthetic reactions are taken to reflect this peculiar nature and to vary accordingly. Nothing in this discussion or the discussion of the *Moderation* allows the reader to entertain the hypothesis that there might be a form of aesthetic response that is universal and that responds to a moral kind of beauty.

The two views of aesthetic experience are not, after all, mutually exclusive; it is possible to hold that certain responses are purely individual while others are universal. In al-Ghazālī's own time, this view was clearly enunciated by a philosopher with whose oeuvre al-Ghazālī had more than a passing acquaintance, Abū ʿAlī Miskawayh (d. 1030). In a compendium of questions and answers exchanged with the litterateur Abū Ḥayyān al-Tawḥīdī (d. 1023), Miskawayh fields a question about what causes us to judge certain kinds of forms beautiful or fine (*istiḥsān al-ṣūra al-ḥasana*). He replies by making a distinction between a "universal and essential" (*dhātī kullī*) response, which we experience towards forms that nature has been most successful in imprinting on matter and that thus correspond most faithfully to the transcendent ideal found in the soul, and a "particular and accidental" (*ʿaraḍī juzʾī*) response that is relative to the (imbalanced) humoural mixture of given individuals. In the latter case, "what one person finds pleasant the other finds repugnant, and vice versa."[24] If al-Ghazālī is aware of this type of possibility, he gives no sign of it, and makes no use of it that would allow us to unify his positions.

In the above, I have helped myself to the labels "moral" and "aesthetic" in distinguishing between the different applications of the term *ḥasan*. This reflects the kind of conceptual distinctions we ourselves find it natural to make on both a theoretical and ordinary-language level. Thus, although I did my best to stick to my principled translation of *ḥasan* as "fine" in the above, this translation comes under strain in *kalām* texts, and in many regards, it seems more natural to translate "good" or "right" in one case and "beautiful" in the other. Yet the terms "moral" and "aesthetic" have no exact counterpart in the parlance of the texts and thinkers we are considering. This raises an important question about the relationship between these two meanings of *ḥusn* which is of immediate relevance for the point under discussion. In what sense *are* they distinct, from the perspective of these thinkers, in the absence of a definite terminological demarcation? Does this assumption reflect our own theoretical and linguistic prejudices rather than real features of the intellectual schemes of these Muslim thinkers? As we saw earlier, this is a question that has a counterpart in the case of the Greek term *kalon*. One argument we reviewed (Irwin's) suggested that Aristotle, for his part, clearly distinguished between two different senses of the word, "morally right" and "beautiful," recognising these as two distinct properties. What about these philosophical speakers of Arabic?

Now it is important to keep in mind that the theological works written by Ashʿarites, Muʿtazilites, and others were polemical in nature, and the positions expressed were always functional to some argumentative end. The argumentative ends of Ashʿarite theologians, as the above makes clear, were best served by refusing to make a strong distinction between different semantic dimensions of the terms *ḥasan* and *qabīḥ*.[25] Things were otherwise for the Muʿtazilites, who, for obvious reasons, were deeply invested in developing that distinction and putting clear blue water between (what we may call) the terms' moral and aesthetic applications. This reflects the important fact that the Muʿtazilites accepted the Ashʿarite understanding of aesthetic experience as relative, idiosyncratic, temperament-based.

In his magnum opus, *The Sufficiency in God's Unity and Justice*, the Baṣran Muʿtazilite thinker ʿAbd al-Jabbār (d. 1025) makes the point by distinguishing between the different objects to which the term *qabīḥ* may be applied—actions on the one hand and physical forms on the other—and between the basis on which it is applied in each case. The application of the term to actions is based on cognitive judgements of desert shared by all people. When an action is called "bad" (*qabīḥ*), this means that a person who freely chooses it deserves blame for performing it unless mitigating circumstances are present. Thus, "every person endowed with reason (*ʿāqil*) knows that someone who commits injustice deserves blame on that account, unless a preventative factor arises." The application of the term to physical forms is based on contingent emotional reactions of repugnance or attraction which vary from person to person and even from time to time. Thus, "a [physical] form is called 'ugly' (*qabīḥ*) insofar as one finds it repugnant to look at it."[26] Especially important is the specific suggestion that ʿAbd al-Jabbār offers about how to understand the relationship between these meanings. He identifies two possible positions: that both meanings are proper or primary (*ḥaqīqa*), and that one is proper and the other figurative or metaphorical (*majāz*). His own stated preference lies with the latter view: it is the meaning that is sound from the perspective of reason (*yaṣiḥḥu ʿaqlan*) that is proper and the term is applied to physical objects by way of resemblance or analogy (*tashabbuh*).[27]

ʿAbd al-Jabbār's definition of the term in its moral sense, of course, reflects the basic commitments of the Muʿtazilites. And taken as an account of ordinary linguistic usage, it was contested by Ashʿarite thinkers (recall al-Ghazālī's account of good and bad as whatever agrees with the speaker's purposes). It is not my concern here to adjudicate between these competing accounts, though at a minimum, we might agree that taking "conformity with a rational perspective" as a criterion is probably not the best methodological foundation for a faithful descriptive account of actual linguistic usage. The important point to notice, however, is that Muʿtazilite thinkers had thus made a distinction between different semantic dimensions of the *ḥasan-qabīḥ* pair, "moral" and "aesthetic," albeit *avant la lettre*. As an Ashʿarite polemicist, al-Ghazālī would likely have been familiar with this way of articulating the distinction. This is what makes it so striking that in his discussion in the *Revival*, he should make no allusion to the issue and give no evidence of recognising that the space for such a distinction might fundamentally exist, let alone provide a principled account of it to vie with the Muʿtazilites'. Doing so, crucially, would have meant forging direct links between the type of discussion taking place in works of dialectical theology and the type of discussion undertaken in the *Revival* and affiliated works.

Al-Ghazālī comes close to offering a principled view of this type of semantic relation in connection with the concept of beauty (*jamāl*), as we saw earlier. Referring to its two applications in the *Exalted Aim*—to outward and inward form—he identifies the latter as a historically posterior semantic expansion. Yet among other things, it is significant that the focus of these comments is the term *jamāl*. This term, as mentioned earlier, featured strongly in texts influenced by philosophical ideas, but it was not the term that organised theological debates about ethics. The key term in these debates was *ḥusn*. In the *Revival*, al-Ghazālī treats the terms *ḥusn* and *jamāl* as interchangeable, often juxtaposing them in the same breath, and he says nothing that would call to mind the special life the former concept had led in theological debates. Above all, he does not engage with the semantic distinctions that certain parties to this debate had made between the ethical and aesthetic applications of this concept. This is also a way of saying that he marks no distinction comparable to Aristotle's, and ultimately provides no explicit account of the relation between the good and the beautiful on our terms.

The effect of this, combined with everything mentioned above, is to make one wonder whether al-Ghazālī was going out of his way to discourage the reader from considering the links between the two contexts represented by his legal/theological and philosophical/Sufi ethical works. And even if we don't go so far as to attribute to him a deliberate intention to thwart certain natural comparisons, the problem is one and the same: the viewpoints expressed by al-Ghazālī in these two separate contexts appear to be in fundamental conflict.

6 Resolving the conflict

An interpretive toolbox

What, then, to make of this problem?

First, it must be observed that this problem forms part of a broader pattern of dissonances between the emphases and assumptions governing al-Ghazālī's two sets of works. The ethical focus of each set—action as the primary object of ethical assessment in one, virtue in the other—is one such dissonance, already mentioned. The present case can be seen as an instance of a larger dissonance between the epistemological assumptions underpinning each set and the different ways they represent the functions and limitations of rational reflection.[1] Here, an acknowledgement of the availability of value (specifically the value of certain kinds of character) to the untutored mind is coupled with an apparently objectivist understanding of that value. The aspects of human character we naturally experience as beautiful are genuine perfections, truly constitutive of (for intellectual virtues) or instrumental to (for moral virtues) the human good.

Some of these emphases channel ideas that had found expression in Hellenistic philosophical texts, whose influence is especially palpable in al-Ghazālī's virtue-centred writings. Seen from this perspective, the present problem would appear to be simply the newest case in a very old file: al-Ghazālī's elusive intellectual relationship to the ideas of the philosophers against whom he famously took up the cudgels in the *Precipitance of the Philosophers*. This question has received considerable attention in recent scholarship from different angles, such as al-Ghazālī's views on prophecy, causality, or the soul. Yet the general problem of how to reconcile the apparently conflicting messages of al-Ghazālī's works was posed far earlier, and was recognised already barely a generation or two after his death by a number of prominent Muslim intellectuals, including Ibn Ṭufayl (d. 1185) and Ibn Rushd (d. 1198).

What approaches have commentators ancient and modern adopted in the face of this general problem, and how can they help resolve the

DOI: 10.4324/9781003196556-6

present one? Here, I will focus on three strategies: chronology, doctrine of discourse, and supercharged hermeneutics.

Chronology

The first strategy is the simplest: it takes the appearance of conflict at face value and postulates that it is the result of intellectual change. This strategy has the virtue of recognising that even the greatest thinkers may change their minds on important issues over their lifetime. This was the solution adopted by Montgomery Watt, for example, when faced with the most philosophical of al-Ghazālī's treatises on ethics, *The Scale of Action*, which he found to be incompatible with the critical view of philosophical ethics he took to be expressed in al-Ghazālī's autobiography, the *Deliverer from Error*. His opinion was that al-Ghazālī likely rejected much of what he had written in that treatise as his enthusiasm for philosophy deflated. The momentous events depicted in the *Deliverer*, where al-Ghazālī chronicles the rupture his social and professional life underwent in 1095 following his dramatic decision to abandon his teaching post and family life in Baghdad and devote himself to the practice of Sufism, have often served as a keystone for this type of interpretation, with his "spiritual conversion" taken to herald seismic changes on an intellectual level.[2]

This understanding of al-Ghazālī's biography has come under heated criticism more recently, and there has been a considerable body of work highlighting the continuity in his intellectual commitments, particularly his commitments to philosophical views (including views on ethics).[3] Yet be that as it may, this strategy is of no help in the present case, for the simple reason that the works in which al-Ghazālī expresses apparently conflicting views resist arrangement in a suitably tidy chronological order. On one widely accepted view, the *Revival* was written after the *Moderation* (which was likely written in the same year as the *Scale*) and before the *Quintessence*.[4] That is, it was sandwiched between two works in which al-Ghazālī appears to defend traditional Ashʿarite views.

Doctrine of discourse

The term was coined by Timothy Gianotti in a book dedicated to settling the fractious question of al-Ghazālī's understanding of the soul as expressed across different works.[5] The concept, however, is much older. On one account, in fact, it was introduced by al-Ghazālī himself in a much-discussed passage at the end of the *Scale*. Asked to state his doctrine (*madhhab*) in the book—is it ranged with Ashʿarite doctrine or with Sufism?[6]—he distinguished between three doctrinal levels, or three senses in which we might speak of a person's doctrine. There's the doctrine to which one pledges allegiance in public disputations, which depends on environmental and geographical contingencies and inherited loyalties (that's how one person ends up a Muʿtazilite, say, and another an Ashʿarite); the doctrine one teaches, which depends on the understanding and capabilities of one's student; and the doctrine one privately believes based on the results of one's own reflective inquiry, which one only shares with those who share one's level of comprehension. Al-Ghazālī concluded with an admonition to inquire into the truth independently and to avoid pre-packaged doctrines.[7]

Numerous commentators past and present, beginning from Ibn Ṭufayl, have converged in regarding this passage as the key for unlocking al-Ghazālī's work and resolving its apparent tensions. From this standpoint, these tensions are no accident, but the result of a deliberate and judiciously chosen method on al-Ghazālī's part. Specifically, the positions that al-Ghazālī expresses need to be considered against the genre of the particular work in which they appear and against al-Ghazālī's reflective view of the nature and function (and hence audience) of that genre. Each genre, Gianotti notes, has its own "parameters and qualifications"; once we have taken stock of this and relativised al-Ghazālī's statements to the relevant genre, "perceived conflicts between statements belonging to separate genres are rendered far less problematic."[8] This hermeneutic incorporates a *pro tanto* commitment to the fundamental consistency of al-Ghazālī's work. In the words of Richard Frank, one of the best-known latter-day exponents of this approach: "There is a basic, integrated theoretical system that underlies al-Ghazālī's logical and theological writings, orders them, and gives them consistency." Al-Ghazālī's oeuvre turns out to be an "essentially consistent, albeit rhetorically modulated, address" to his intellectual community.[9]

This obviously requires a careful sorting of the different genres that al-Ghazālī plied, a task that both Frank and Gianotti undertake. Without going into the details, I will mention one shared element of their analysis, and this is the emphasis on the epistemic limitations of one specific discourse, namely, dialectical theology (*kalām*). Dialectical theology, in al-Ghazālī's view, has indeed a legitimate function in the religious community, to defend correct theological doctrine against heresy. Yet its role is purely defensive, and its disputational character and dialectical reliance on *endoxa* (*mashhūrāt*) make it a poor instrument for the discovery of truth (*kashf al-ḥaqāʾiq wa-maʿrifatuhā ʿalā mā hiya ʿalayhi*).[10] The inferior epistemic status of theological works is reflected in the profile of their intended audience. Frank describes both the *Moderation* and the *Jerusalem Epistle*—the short theological tract incorporated in the *Revival*—as "lower-level handbooks" for "simple, uneducated people."[11] In Frank's view, al-Ghazālī's theological works are Ashʿarite solely in veneer and camouflage his true metaphysics, which rather owes to Avicenna. If we wish to hear al-Ghazālī's real views, we should look away from his theological works.

Now how might this help us approach our present question? Following the example of these commentators, one obvious possibility would be to query the depth of al-Ghazālī's commitment to the viewpoint on ethics expressed in his theological works (or the theological segments embedded within his works of legal theory, such as the *Quintessence*). Here is one way of fleshing out this possibility more concretely. Perhaps we should distinguish between the propositions that constitute the true creed defended in *kalām* works—and it seems we must uphold al-Ghazālī's commitment to the truth of *that*[12]—and between the arguments used in such works to defend them. Perhaps al-Ghazālī's rejection of ethical rationalism and objectivism should be seen as merely dialectical: a claim he thought *effective* for defending the proposition that really mattered, but not necessarily *true*. The proposition that really mattered is that God is not subject to obligation. It was this proposition that Muʿtazilites had denied, and their claims about ethical rationalism and objectivism had also been developed in a functional relationship to it.[13]

I will be returning to this last proposal shortly from another direction. Yet how satisfying does this view seem in the present context? On the one hand, it will resonate with those of us who have often been beset by a not dissimilar suspicion of dialectical theology as a genre, and who have wondered how its rigid rules of operation and artificial polarities of polemical engagement affected the spirit in which inquiry was pursued, and whether they supported the intellectual qualities required for the best sort of inquiry to flourish, such as good faith, open-mindedness, and intellectual honesty. (This would also be al-Ghazālī's moral complaint against dialectical theology: that it fosters a pernicious pride and love of glory.) This translates into a sneaking suspicion that perhaps theologians did not always *quite* believe the things they declared to great fanfare.

But there is a more germane observation.[14] Because if we are to take the genre of writing in which certain claims appear as a basis for qualifying the epistemic status of these claims, this needs to be done consistently. This means that we also need to take into account the nature of the competing genre (or discourse, given its mould-breaking qualities) in the case we are considering, the one represented by the *Revival*. Now certainly the *Revival* is a work that is more hand-over-heart in certain obvious ways. It is literally a guide to matters of the heart, and its mission is to guide its readers along the *true* road to the *true* salvation. Importantly, the *Revival* also internally includes an evaluation of different discourses (a topic of book 1, *On Knowledge*), and internally declares its superiority to the discourses of dialectical theology and law. There is a nice analogy here: just as law (*fiqh*) does not deliver the highest form of *practical* knowledge required for this spiritual journey (what al-Ghazālī calls *ʿilm al-muʿāmala*), so dialectical theology does not deliver the highest form of *metaphysical* knowledge (what he calls *ʿilm al-mukāshafa*).

Yet the rub is that the *Revival* does not take it upon itself to provide the latter kind of knowledge either, often alluding to it but always hastily pulling down the veil over it, in a constant and provocative exercise of self-limitation. Its stated province is the domain of the practical. In Gianotti's description (echoing many other readers'), the *Revival* is "designed to be a detailed and accessible handbook for human perfection."[15] Its goal is to help its readers become better people—the kind of people they need to be in order to achieve ultimate happiness. This practical aim explains the overall "non-confrontational style" of the book, as Taneli Kukkonen has observed, which makes al-Ghazālī steer clear of the more pugilistic treatment of abstract issues that typifies his theological and legal works.[16] While al-Ghazālī does deal with a host of issues on higher-level terms (the account of love we have seen is a prime example), he does so within the more-or-less firm boundaries dictated by his practical aims.

Now clearly, al-Ghazālī needs to tell his readers what (he believes) represents the *true* road to happiness. But that is eminently compatible with not telling them the whole truth, and sticking to the truths that are absolutely essential on a strict need-to-know basis. Readers looking to mend their souls, for example, don't need to understand the true nature of the soul (*ḥaqīqatuhā fī dhātihā*); they only need to understand its qualities and states (*ṣifatuhā wa-aḥwāluhā*).[17] And here is a key point to consider. In the polemical discussions of ethics featured in his theological (and legal) works, al-Ghazālī had ultimately conceded to the Muʿtazilites that ordinary people make apparently deontological moral judgements and even choose to act in certain ways that do not appear to serve their interest and potentially conflict with it. (Even minds bent to the rigid rules of operation and artificial polarities of polemical engagement of *kalām* eventually had to acknowledge such empirical phenomena.) This was the newest and most devastating Ashʿarite strategy: grant that people make such judgements and perform such actions, but question what *really* stands behind them. As al-Ghazālī put it in the *Quintessence*, "we do not deny that such judgements are widespread among people and are praiseworthy and widely accepted (*maḥmūda mashhūra*)"; rather we deny their foundation (*mustanad*). His ruthless analysis had suggested that this foundation was invariably egoism, suitably harnessed and moulded by psychological and social processes.[18] To use a modern expression, the al-Ghazālī of the *Moderation* and the *Quintessence* subscribed to the "veneer theory" of morals. Al-Ghazālī's more immediate frame of reference was Avicenna's analysis of moral judgements as widely accepted propositions (*endoxa* or *mashhūrāt*). Yes, people widely make such judgements, but this says nothing about their epistemic credentials. It would certainly be a mistake to assume such judgements are grounded in pure reason, as the Muʿtazilites alleged.[19]

With this in mind, al-Ghazālī's discussion of moral beauty may appear in a new light. Given the practical aims of the *Revival*, is it not conceivable that al-Ghazālī may have weighed the options and decided that from a pedagogical perspective, the moral *endoxa* were best left untouched? That the best course was to leave his readers to the phenomena—to their ordinary moral reactions—and to draw a veil of silence over his higher-level view of their true nature and foundation, as revealed in his works of Ashʿarite theology? Between Muʿtazilite moral objectivism and the Ashʿarite deconstructive alternative, it's not hard to say which meta-ethical position is likely to have better results on the plane of concrete ethical practice. That, for example, was the reason one later thinker, the Ḥanbalite theologian Ibn Taymiyya (d. 1328), would take up arms against the Ashʿarite position: it makes for bad ethics (or what's the same, bad religion).[20] If you think "good" picks out a real property, you're more likely to do it.

Thus, one genre seems too dialectical, the other too practical, to supply an expression of the undiluted truth. Is this the final word to be pronounced on the topic? I am not too sure. It is not clear to me, for example, whether the hypothesis just outlined—that al-Ghazālī stood by the Ashʿarite view of value in the *Revival* but calculatingly suppressed it for pedagogical reasons—is entirely consistent with the role the antagonistic claims are asked to play in the *Revival*. We may remember that the human reaction to ethical value (moral beauty) serves al-Ghazālī as a basis for articulating an ideal of the superior form of love we can and should direct to God. Within al-Ghazālī's scheme, there could be few higher spiritual stakes. Similarly, in this part of his discussion, al-Ghazālī does not merely let common intuitions be—he enthusiastically embellishes them in calligraphic print. His affirmation of the existence of a disinterested form of love is simply too strong and explicit.

There is other evidence one could consider from both sides. In short, the argument is not over. What my brief discussion at the very least suggests is that this argument is complex and any solution is unlikely to please all parties.

Supercharged hermeneutics

For certain of al-Ghazālī's readers, this type of strategy is inherently dissatisfactory and should be avoided at all costs. Frank Griffel, for example, has objected to the use of al-Ghazālī's remarks in the *Scale* as an interpretive key to his project, particularly when coupled with a division of his works into the "esoteric" and "exoteric." Such approaches are usually both a consequence and a cause of shirking the duties of interpretation. As he acerbically puts it:

> Often, assigning esotericism to an author or referring to inconsistencies in a textual corpus is a hermeneutic device to mask the failure of interpreters to understand the texts ... A good interpretation readily admits the lacunae in its understanding. Only such a frank admission will encourage us to work harder, to read these texts again and again, and to consider new levels of meaning that might reconcile apparent contradictions. Thus, finding such contradictions should lead us to take these texts more—and not less—seriously.[21]

Instead of using the dates or genres of particular works to discount their content, we should roll up our sleeves and supercharge our efforts to come up with interpretations of the content that allow us to reconcile any conflicting messages. This hermeneutic, it will be clear, also departs from a commitment to consistency. Applied to the vexed question of al-Ghazālī's understanding of causality, Griffel discovers this consistency in an attitude of agnosticism— itself not at odds with Ashʿarite epistemology—between the two competing metaphysical explanations, Ashʿarite and Avicennan. "Although both theories offer possible and consistent explanations of God's creative activity," according to al-Ghazālī "neither of them can be demonstratively proven." Importantly, whatever the metaphysical truth of the matter, it leaves our practical life untouched, and we can still carry on thinking and talking about causes and effects as we ordinarily do, that is to say, as if they were inseparably linked.[22]

My decision to leave this approach till last should not be taken to suggest that we should treat this option as the last resort. On the contrary, I agree with Griffel that it ought to be the first. It is simply that I am not confident that I have a robust proposal for the present case that can be comfortably fitted under this description. In practice, it is not clear to me that we can neatly separate this supercharged interpretive approach from the discourse-centred approach outlined above. Interpretation makes reference to aims and intentions, and a description of an author's ends will often coincide at least in part with a description of the ends he had as a typical contributor to a particular genre. This point is relevant for considering one proposal I would like to cautiously put forward as a possible contender (if not a perfect fit for this category) for removing the contradiction I have plotted between al-Ghazālī's ethical views as expressed in the *Revival* and his views as expressed in his theological and legal works.

I hypothesised earlier that al-Ghazālī's rejection of Muʿtazilite-style ethical rationalism and objectivism may have been merely dialectical, an expedient for defending the theological tenet that really mattered and that he genuinely believed to be true. This was the tenet that God's freedom is not subject to any limitations that might derive from homegrown human concepts of right and wrong. The rallying cry, ever since al-Ashʿarī (d. 935), was that God is under no *sharīʿa*. "There is no-one above him to permit or command, restrain or prohibit, prescribe rules and impose limits."[23] He is not subject to obligation (*wujūb*), not subject to human claims (*ḥaqq*); there is nothing he *ought* to do and could be reproved for failing to do. Reason bothered the Ashʿarites mainly insofar as it was the source of bombastic anthropocentric claims about God's obligations. The Ashʿarite analysis of key moral terms like "obligatory," "good" and "bad," or more substantively, "unjust," accordingly served to show why they are inapplicable to God and invalid as sources of normative restriction on his activity. God transcends human measurements. A glance at the location where these ethical questions were discussed in al-Ghazālī's and his fellow-theologians' *kalām* works already tells half the story: they appear under the rubric of God's acts. A glance at the titles of the subsections, corresponding to the propositions under defence, tells the other half. In the *Moderation*, they include: "That God is *not* obliged to do what is optimal for human beings," "That God is *not* obliged to reward human beings if he imposes obligations on them and they obey him," "That God has the *right* to impose obligations on human beings that they can but also cannot fulfil."

Yet if this was the fundamental concern of Ashʿarite theology in the question of ethics, we could perhaps see why a thinker like al-Ghazālī might have been prepared to acknowledge the evaluative insights of human reason so long as this did not appear to carry the same problematic implications. Unlike theological and legal literature, where the concept of duty or obligation reigns supreme, shadowed by its alter ago the concept of prohibition,[24] in virtue literature across its different forms—especially philosophical, but not exclusively—the evaluative emphasis is different. The objects of ethical attention, the virtues, present as beautiful (*jamīl*) or noble, commanding love and admiration. (*Makārim al-akhlāq*, "the noble traits of character," was a common designation in less philosophical texts on the virtues). The evaluative register, to adapt Henry Sidgwick's expression, carries "attractive" rather than "imperative" force; it centres less on the right than on the good.[25]

This point has sometimes been used to draw a broad contrast between the moral theories of ancient philosophers such as Plato and Aristotle and many modern theories. The former, Aryeh Kosman observes, "are essentially informed by their allegiance to a notion of the good rooted in what we are attracted to rather than to a notion of the good rooted in a concept of the right." For Kosman, this general point flows out of a reflection on the place of the *kalon* in their theories, with its melting rainbow of aesthetic-moral connotations. Among these philosophers, "the moral sphere is governed by a principle … clearly cousin-german to the beautiful. And when we recall that it has a foundation, shared by the *kalon* and the beautiful alike, in the faces of the young and fair, we will recognize this principle as specifically erotic—rooted in what we are attracted to."[26]

The contrast between a "morality of attraction" and "a morality of right," to be sure, should not be drawn too sharply, as Kosman himself emphasises. Among these philosophers, the sense of attraction or desire is after all informed by reason, which instructs us to desire appropriately. Yet even taken loosely, this contrast may be helpful in trying to understand how an intellectual like al-Ghazālī, as he negotiated two types of ethical literature characterised by divergent evaluative registers and emphases—the theological-legal literature centring on action and duty (a morality of right) and the philosophical literature centring on virtue and beauty (a morality of attraction)—may have concluded that he could safely endorse the perspective of the latter without prejudice to his fundamental theological concerns.[27] Reason acknowledges certain qualities of character as real perfections. Yet this is an acknowledgement of a natural object of love rather than a normative constraint. Moreover, in al-Ghazālī's appropriation of the philosophical-Sufi topos of *Imitatio Dei*, it is God who forms the true object of such love and also the standard of the virtues. It is God that measures and constrains us, rather than the other way around, as Muʿtazilite thinkers had appeared to argue. The standard of virtue is transcendent. Al-Ghazālī's concern with preserving God's transcendence is thus fully satisfied within this paradigm and remains the constant that holds both his theological-legal works and his virtue-ethical works together.[28]

It may be counted as more than circumstantial evidence in favour of this view that we find a related pattern in the work of Ibn Taymiyya, an avid reader of al-Ghazālī's oeuvre and undeclared re-articulator of some of his trademark ideas. Ibn Taymiyya, for his part, offers far more vocal support to a *seemingly* Muʿtazilite-style view of ethics; and in his account, it is an overwhelming focus on the evaluative register of the "good" (*ḥasan*) as against the "obligatory" (*wājib*) that turns out to grease the wheels and remove any theological friction this view might create for his own fundamental theological concern with God's transcendence.[29]

Whether the two concepts—and the overall moral paradigms they are associated with—*can* be plausibly pulled apart seems even more open to question in al-Ghazālī's case than in Aristotle and Plato's. Vice, after all, leads to harm, in al-Ghazālī's view; and as we briefly saw, in his theological-legal works he had recognised that, in a basic sense, acts are designated as "obligatory" insofar as failure to perform them would expose the person to harm. In that sense, the acquisition of virtue is also obligatory. Yet we may note that in his theological-legal works, al-Ghazālī, like many of his fellow-Ashʿarites, had laid emphasis on one particular type of harm, obtaining in the otherworldly realm. It is this that he had most strongly insisted human beings only know about through scripture, which communicates the fact that God attached certain kinds of otherworldly consequences (viz., punishment) to certain acts and in doing so rendered them obligatory.[30] This suggests another hypothesis as to why al-Ghazālī may not have viewed the account of moral beauty he presented in the *Revival* as incompatible with his account of ethics in those other works. What he affirmed in his discussion of love in the *Revival* was our natural ability to recognise and respond to the beauty of virtue. But the insight that a certain state of character is admirable is logically separable from the insight that it is conducive to certain metaphysical outcomes. (As al-Ghazālī puts it pithily albeit metaphorically in one place: the vices are "gateways that open out to God's burning Fire" while the virtues are "gateways of the heart that open out to the bliss of paradise."[31]) Just because we experience a certain quality as beautiful, it need not mean we understand *why* it merits this response—that is to say, why it is a true virtue or perfection. The more basic point that our emotional reactions to moral excellence, notably admiration, may require a certain type of cognitive processing or reflective articulation before we can identify their objects is something that a number of contemporary philosophers would be prepared recognise.[32] In al-Ghazālī's case, the key issue would be less about identifying what we admire than why we ought to. The latter is an explanation that belongs (at least in part) to the sphere of higher-level metaphysical theorising, along with a number of other claims, notably al-Ghazālī's claim that what makes a certain quality a virtue is its being a virtue in God.[33]

This, of course, serves to underline the fact that our natural reactions are fallible and corrigible. Our intuitive judgements may stand to be revised once informed by this higher-level understanding. Al-Ghazālī does not go out of his way to emphasise this point in his discussion of moral beauty in the *Revival*, as mentioned earlier, but perhaps we need to assume it is working in the background if we are to weave everything into a coherent whole. Our natural reason-based reactions require correction from scripture. This is the very kind of correction we may see al-Ghazālī as supplying in the *Revival* both by expanding the roster of substantive virtues to include not just the philosophers' (wisdom, courage, temperance, justice, and their subdivisions) but also the mystics' (such as gratitude, trust, or love in God), and by offering higher-level explanations of the nature of virtue and its metaphysical foundations. That reason (or nature) is completed by scripture is a claim on which even the al-Ghazālī of the *Moderation* and the *Quintessence* would have been happy to sign off.

Read in this manner, the conflict begins to melt away. Is this hermeneutics one charge too far—hermeneutics on steroids? I will leave this to readers to judge.

7 Concluding comment

There are, no doubt, other explanations and interpretive proposals that could be developed to clear up the puzzle I picked out. Yet I will stop here, leaving this task to al-Ghazālī's many other dedicated readers. On the relationship between the different parts of the universe of al-Ghazālī's oeuvre, it will be impossible to ever have the last word.

The question pursued above, as will be clear, stems from a fundamentally interpretive concern about how to unify al-Ghazālī's ethical thinking. This type of question is hard to avoid to the extent that we seek to understand a thinker as a whole and we are naturally driven to scrutinise the relationship between the different ideas he has expressed. If our main interest lies in exploring the development of one of these ideas on its own terms, on the other hand, our ability to resolve such questions will seem of secondary importance.

This study has been guided by both kinds of concern. But one of its chief aims was to recover al-Ghazālī's account of moral beauty with a view to enriching the historical resources we look back to and situate ourselves against when we seek to rearticulate the relationship between the good and the beautiful, ethics and aesthetics. This relationship, as mentioned earlier, has come under a sharp spotlight among philosophers recently, and there have been incisive new efforts to take possession of it. In Arabo-Islamic culture, as in Greek culture, it was a relationship that was firmly embedded within the givens of language. Should we regard that as a pure coincidence? This is a large question that I cannot tackle as such, but I will draw on one of Kosman's observations in connection with the Greek case to provide a more modest final reflection.

Commenting on the opposition between the terms *kalon* and *aischron* found in Plato's *Gorgias*, Kosman points out that the latter is less about being "ugly" than about being "shameful." The argument of the *Gorgias* reveals "that these concepts are together importantly situated in the register of honor and shame, and what this means more generally is that

DOI: 10.4324/9781003196556-7

they are in the register of our appearance to one another."[1] In Kosman's view, it is the notion of "appearance," taken in the broad sense of "presentation to subjective awareness," that gives us the key to unlocking the larger ethical conception that is reflected in the complex semantic profile of the term *kalon*. In particular, it reveals the close connection between ontology and phenomenology, being and appearance. We moderns "tend to think of beauty in cosmetic terms, as though it concerned always and only a superficial façade of being," which is linked to the fact that we tend to think of appearance as at the very least independent and separate from being, in the best case failing to represent it, in the worst falsifying it. It is this tendency that surfaced at an earlier moment of our discussion when we found ourselves querying the idea that the desire for beauty could be an appropriate sort of moral motivation ("isn't it a desire to *appear* a certain way, rather than to *be* a certain kind of person?"). Things are different with Plato:

> [F]or Plato, appearance is not something separate from being, but simply the presentation of what is to a subject: being, as we say, making its appearance. It is not therefore essentially deceptive; the phenomenological is not standardly the illusion of being ... face not as façade, but as organic expression. The *kalon* in turn reveals the integrity of being and its proper appearance; it constitutes the virtue of proper and expressive appearance ... The *kalon* is, then, not something in addition to the good, and so to speak on its surface. It is the mode of the good that shows forth; it is the splendor of the appearance of the good. The *kalon*, we might say, is the splendid virtue of appearance.[2]

Kosman does not speculate on what caused the displacement of this understanding on a historical level. But in isolating social reactions of honour and shame as the location where the moral-aesthetic meanings of *kalon* come together, he indicates one possible way of understanding the genealogy (in some sense of this word) of its composite profile, and why we should perhaps not be surprised to see it replicated in the evaluative language of other moral communities where such reactions play a prominent regulative role.

Taken as ideal types, such communities are sometimes termed "shame cultures," most basically defined by their preoccupation with the achievement of social status and public esteem. Shame, as Bernard Williams has pointed out, bears a special relation to sight and hence appearance. "The basic experience connected with shame is that of being seen, inappropriately, by the wrong people, in the wrong condition," and its motivations always make reference to "an idea of the gaze of another"—though in its most developed forms, this will be the imagined gaze of an idealised observer.[3] Heroic societies with an aristocratic warrior class tend to be shame cultures, as Peter Hacker notes, governed by a moral code whose central values include military prowess, generosity, hospitality to guests, and the zealous defence of one's honour against slight.[4] Homeric society is often taken as a textbook case of such a culture, whose moral framework—including its concern with status, honour, and appearance and its characteristic fusion of moral and physical excellence into a unitary ideal (*kalokagathia*)—lived on in later Greek culture, though subjected to important renegotiations at the hands of Athenian intellectuals. A similar preoccupation with honour and shame, joined to a heroic code defined by similar values, has commonly been taken to characterise pre-Islamic Arabian society. And just as in the Homeric case, the latter maintained a literary presence in the Islamic world that ensured its continuing cultural influence, albeit in modified form.[5]

In light of Kosman's discussion, it may seem paradoxical to observe that al-Ghazālī in fact shares the distrust of appearances Kosman attributes to us moderns. For al-Ghazālī, the social reactions that our actions attract have a morally corrosive effect, often leading us to pursue appearance at the expense of being. This is the running theme of two books of the *Revival* dedicated to the study of the vices of a concern with appearance: pride, conceit, the quest for honour and standing.[6] Appearance can be falsified; being and appearance often come apart. In al-Ghazālī's account of love, by contrast, we see this chasm sealed, with virtue allowed the peculiar splendour of its appearance. Al-Ghazālī's philosophical view that beauty simply *is* perfection perceived encapsulates directly his commitment to the fundamental unity between how things are and how they appear. The two perspectives can be reconciled on one level by distinguishing between the moral subject with whom they are principally concerned: it is legitimate to admire virtue in others, but not to desire such admiration for one's own. They can also be reconciled on another level by noting that even where al-Ghazālī takes a negative view of appearances, it is not that the concern with appearances has entirely gone away; it is only that the relevant observer has been replaced. What matters is not our appearance to other members of the human community and the reactions of shame and honour with which they receive us. What matters is our appearance before God. This is the subject of another book of the *Revival*, dedicated to the practice of vigilance and self-examination, which teaches readers how to hold themselves in the perpetual consciousness of God's awareness.

From the perspective of the cultural transitions evoked above, the displacement of the concern with social status and public honour by a concern with the esteem meted out by God can be seen as one of the central modifications of the pre-Islamic moral code effected by Muslim intellectuals—even if, as al-Ghazālī's strictures suggest, human nature being what it is, this normative displacement was less than completely realised in actual practice. This displacement, from public esteem to the voice of conscience coinciding with the all-seeing eye of God, is in fact one of several indices often invoked to articulate the difference between shame culture and its other, that is, "guilt culture." Another concerns the primary focus of moral attention. Where the former type of culture prizes ways of being, the latter prizes ways of doing. As Peter Hacker puts it: "The form of the dominant norms of a shame-culture determine what one ought *to be* ... The form of the dominant norms of a guilt-culture is the imperative or dominative tense ('thou shalt'), which determines what one is obligated *to do*. This is the typical form of the obligation-imposing laws of God."[7]

As Hacker emphasises, this contrast should not be taken simplistically. To do so, after all, would be to overlook the well-attested interest taken in moral character among many religious traditions. Certainly, it would be a mistake to foreclose questions about how best to understand the relation between this interest and the equally well-attested interest in right action within such traditions. These are questions, as we have seen, that come up internally within al-Ghazālī's ethics given the different paradigms of ethical reflection that find expression in different parts of his oeuvre: one (expressed in his theological and legal works) shaped by an emphasis on duty, action, and obedience, the other (expressed in a different set of ethical works) shaped by an emphasis on beauty, character, and love. Reading this relation requires us to keep an open mind, and to remain sensitive to many possible layers of explanation. Yet however we read it in this case—whether as a reflection of al-Ghazālī's changing commitments or negotiation of different audiences, as the result of a broader cultural struggle to integrate the different intellectual frameworks (Hellenistic, pre-Islamic Arab, scriptural Islamic, and others) that gave Islamic culture its materials, and/or as a particular stage in the confrontation of a shame-centric culture and a guilt-centric one—it suggests that there is much to learn from this exercise that can enrich the historical context against which we understand the longstanding connection between the beautiful and the good.

For a deeper understanding of the social, cultural, and other processes that may underwrite the linguistic connection between the beautiful and the good more widely across history, we would do well to look to anthropology and studies of linguistic etymology. Taking all these resources together and joining them to a study of these ideas as they have been unfolded historically, we may be able to set the relation between ethics and aesthetics on new foundations and find fresh ways of articulating its truth.

Distinguishing between the different reasons that might motivate the study of history, Nietzsche isolated a type of study one might pursue "as a being who acts and strives," whose hallmark is its quest for "models, teachers, comforters" and images of greatness to serve the purposes of action and life. The ruling commandment for this form of study is: "that which in the past was able to expand the concept 'man' and make it more beautiful must exist everlastingly, so as to be able to accomplish this everlastingly."[8] Looking back, there will obviously be many such concepts, not all of which Nietzsche would have been equally happy to acknowledge as images of human beauty and greatness. Though the history of great exemplars is not the history of ideas, many of us who study the latter are driven by a hope that such ideas might bring beauty closer. And for this, no offer of intellectual fellowship is worth refusing.

Notes

Section 1

1. In the epigram, I rely on the translation of the *Symposium* by Reginald E. Allen (New Haven, CT: Yale University Press, 1993).
2. The quote is from Jan A. Aersten, *Medieval Philosophy and The Transcendentals: The Case of Thomas Aquinas* (Leiden: E.J. Brill, 1996), though Aersten himself isolates *kalokagathia* as the relevant notion in this context. Just how to understand the Janus-faced nature of the term *kalon*, and how to handle the challenges it poses on translation level, is a question that still attracts debate. Good starting points for considering these questions are Terence H. Irwin, "The Sense and Reference of *Kalon* in Aristotle," *Classical Philology* 105 (2010), 381–396 (Special Issue: *Beauty, Harmony, and the Good*, ed. Elizabeth Asmi), and Aryeh Kosman, "Beauty and the Good: Situating the *Kalon*," *Classical Philology* 105 (2010), 341–357.
3. Kosman, "Beauty and the Good," 344, though this remark reflects a particular dialectical stage of his discussion, and Kosman himself is not arguing this gulf. Cf. Irwin's related remarks in "Sense and Reference," 381–382.
4. Panos Paris, "On Form, and the Possibility of Moral Beauty," *Metaphilosophy* 49 (2018), 711–729.
5. Berys Gaut, *Art, Emotion and Ethics* (Oxford: Oxford University Press, 2007), 117; Colin McGinn, *Ethics, Evil, and Fiction* (Oxford: Oxford University Press, 1999), 98–99.
6. Charlotte Brontë, *Jane Eyre* (New York and London: W. W. Norton & Company, 2001), 62.
7. David Hume, *Treatise of Human Nature*, ed. L. A. Selby-Bigge, rev. P. H. Nidditch (Oxford: Clarendon Press, 1978, 2nd edn), 470.
8. On the *Symposium*, see Dimitri Gutas, "Plato's *Symposion* in the Arabic Tradition," *Oriens* 31 (1988), 36–60, and for a general survey of the reception of Platonic writings, idem, "Platon. Tradition arabe," in *Dictionnaire des Philosophes Antiques*, vol. Va, ed. Richard Goulet (Paris: Centre National de la Recherche Scientifique, 2012), 845–863. For the *Theology of Aristotle*, see Peter Adamson, *The Arabic Plotinus: A Study of* The Theology of Aristotle (London: Duckworth, 2002).
9. Two gateway discussions of this theme in Sufi thought are Kazuyo Murata, *Beauty in Sufism: The Teachings of Rūzbihān Baqlī* (Albany, NY: State University of New York Press, 2017) and Cyrus Ali Zargar,

Sufi Aesthetics: Beauty, Love, and the Human Form in Ibn Arabi and 'Iraqi (Columbia, SC: University of South Carolina Press, 2011). See also, with a broader brush, William C. Chittick's brief but illuminating meditation, "The Aesthetics of Islamic Ethics," in *Sharing Poetic Expressions: Beauty, Sublime, Mysticism in Islamic and Occidental Culture*, ed. Anna-Teresa Tymieniecka (Dordrecht; New York: Springer, 2011), 3–14, whose themes intersect especially closely with those of the present study.

10. Existing discussions of this theme of al-Ghazālī's work include Binyamin Abrahamov, *Divine Love in Islamic Mysticism: The Teachings of Al-Ghazâlî and Al-Dabbâgh* (London; New York: Routledge, 2003), Chapter 2; Richard Ettinghausen, "Al-Ghazzālī on Beauty," in *Fine Arts of Islamic Civilization*, ed. Muḥammad Abdul Jabbar Beg (Cambridge: M. A. J. Beg, 2006), 25–36; Carole Hillenbrand, "Some Aspects of al-Ghazālī's Views on Beauty," in *Gott ist schön und Er liebt die Schönheit (God is Beautiful and He Loves Beauty)*, ed. Alma Giese and J. Christoph Bürgel (Bern: Peter Lang, 1994), 249–265; Taneli Kukkonen, "The Good, the Beautiful and the True: Aesthetical Issues in Islamic Philosophy," *Studia Orientalia* 111 (2011), 87–103; Simon Van Den Bergh, "The 'Love of God' in al-Ghazālī's *Vivification of Theology*," *Journal of Semitic Studies* 1 (1956), 305–321; Mohamed Ahmed Sherif, *Ghazālī's Theory of Virtue* (Albany, NY: State University of New York Press, 1975), 145–153; and José Miguel Puerta Vílchez, *Aesthetics in Arabic Thought from Pre-Islamic Arabia through al-Andalus*, trans. Consuelo López-Morillas (Leiden; Boston, MA: Brill, 2017), Chapter 3.7.

Section 2

1. There have been a number of recent studies and survey pieces exploring the status of aesthetics in Arabic-Islamic culture more generally and philosophical culture more particularly. They include Deborah L. Black, "Aesthetics in Islamic Philosophy," in *Routledge Encyclopedia of Philosophy*, ed. Edward Craig (London; New York: Routledge, 1998), 75–79; Samir Mahmoud, "Beauty and Aesthetics in Classical Islamic Thought: An Introduction," *Kalam Journal* 1 (2018), 7–21; Valerie Gonzalez, "Beauty and Aesthetic Experience in Classical Arabic Thought," in *Beauty in Islam: Aesthetics in Islamic Art and Architecture* (London: I.B. Tauris, 2001); Aaron Hughes, "'God is Beautiful and Loves Beauty': The Role of Aesthetics in Medieval Islamic and Jewish Philosophy," in *The Texture of the Divine: Imagination in Medieval Islamic and Jewish Thought* (Bloomington; Indianapolis, IN: Indiana University Press, 2004); Doris Behrens-Abouseif, *Beauty in Arabic Culture* (Princeton, NJ: Markus Wiener, 1998); Oliver Leaman, *Islamic Aesthetics* (Edinburgh: Edinburgh University Press, 2004); and Vílchez, *Aesthetics in Arabic Thought*.
2. A recognition that I will here assume does not presuppose agreement on definitional questions such as what makes an experience, attitude, or property aesthetic, at least when it comes to core cases such as the ones discussed next in the main text. These definitional questions remain open to philosophical debate.

3. Al-Ghazālī, *The Revival of the Religious Sciences/Iḥyāʾ ʿulūm al-dīn* (Cairo: Lajnat Nashr al-Thaqāfa al-Islāmiyya, 1356–1357 AH [1937–1938]), 9: 1736; I cite this edition based on the pagination of the Dar al-Shaʿb edition (n.d.).
4. Above all, the pleasure appears to attach to the object simply insofar as it is seen or heard, and not insofar as it might serve as a means for satisfying some other desire; we don't go on to eat the vegetation and we don't take pleasure in the birdsong as an indication of where to point our hunting weapon. Al-Ghazālī's entire point (which requires him to single out the most inoffensive forms of sensory pleasure) pivots on that basis.
5. For some extra comment on this point from the perspective of al-Ghazālī's understanding of virtue, see my "Does al-Ghazālī Have a Theory of Virtue?" in *Mysticism and Ethics in Islam*, ed. Bilal Orfali, Mohammed Rustom, and Atif Khalil (Beirut: American University of Beirut Press, forthcoming).
6. *The Scale of Action/Mīzān al-ʿamal*, ed. Sulaymān Dunyā (Cairo: Dār al-Maʿārif, 1964), 310–311; cf. 299: "anything that helps satisfy the needs of the present world also helps with the next, as the next world is reached through these worldly means."
7. *Iḥyāʾ*, 15: 2833. Al-Ghazālī's *The Wisdom in God's Creation/al-Ḥikma fī makhlūqāt Allāh* can be read as a companion piece to this book of the *Revival*, as can the earlier book dedicated to the topic of gratitude (and patience: *Kitab al-Ṣabr waʾl-shukr*), though its specific focus is on the created order *qua* beneficial. For a comment on the *Book of Contemplation* from a different direction, see Binyamin Abrahamov, "Al-Ghazālī and the Rationalization of Sufism," in *Islam and Rationality: The Impact of al-Ghazālī*, vol. 1, ed. Georges Tamer (Leiden: Brill, 2015), 35–48, though Abrahamov's "syllogistic thinking" as a translation for *tafakkur* seems too narrow to capture the more empirically oriented type of inquiry al-Ghazālī considers under this heading. This empirical dimension is also Ahmed El Shamsy's emphasis in his remarks on *al-Ḥikma fī makhlūqāt Allāh* in the context of a broader argument in "The Wisdom of God's Law: Two Theories," in *Islamic Law in Theory: Studies in Jurisprudence in Honor of Bernard Weiss*, ed. Robert Gleave and Kevin Reinhart (Leiden: Brill, 2014), 19–37; see esp. 32–33.
8. Al-Ghazālī's taxonomy of the different types of relationship in which we may stand to our physical needs and their material in *Iḥyāʾ*, 15: 2755–2756, offers a helpful though partial compass for thinking through this question.
9. See Hillebrand, "Some Aspects," 257; the *Revival*'s dedicated discussion of the topic takes place in book 18. Al-Ghazālī's attitude to music has complex roots and reflects a philosophical view that found notable expression in the work of the Ikhwān al-Ṣafāʾ.

Section 3

1. Immanuel Kant, *Critique of the Power of Judgment*, trans. Paul Guyer and Eric Matthews (Cambridge: Cambridge University Press, 2000), 154. For a fuller development of this observation, see Robert R. Clewis, *The Kantian Sublime and the Revelation of Freedom* (Cambridge: Cambridge University Press, 2009), especially Chapter 2.3.

2. See Arthur Schopenhauer, *The World as Will and Representation*, trans. E. F. J. Payne (New York: Dover Publications, 1966), 1: 206–207.
3. Irwin, "Sense and Reference," 381.
4. Ibid, 395.
5. Though *jamāl* is more hospitable to the latter, more aesthetically valenced two options. As Franz Rosenthal points out, there is a small minority of words denoting what is good or excellent that cannot be used in an aesthetic sense ("On Art and Aesthetics in Graeco-Arabic Wisdom Literature," in his *Four Essays on Art and Literature in Islam* [Leiden: Brill, 1971], 12). *Jayyid* is one example; *khayr* is another. From the other direction, Doris Behrens-Abouseif notes that there are a few terms that denote physical beauty which do not admit a moral application, such as *malīḥ* or *wasīm* (*Beauty in Arabic Culture*, 17). Be that as it may, the evidence both of ordinary language and of intellectual articulations such as those we will be considering here weighs heavily against her surprising claim concerning "the separation between the good and the beautiful in Arabic culture" (ibid, 8). Speculating on the question which sense—moral or aesthetic—was historically prior, Rosenthal draws on the evidence of Akkadian to suggest that in at least one case, *jamīl*, it was the former, and that the original meaning of the word was "obliging," "kind," and the like ("Art and Aesthetics," 12–13).
6. Al-Rāghib al-Iṣfahānī, *An Exposition of the Obscure Terms of the Qurʾan/Mufradāt fī gharīb al-Qurʾān*, ed. Ṣafwān ʿAdnān Dawūdī (Damascus: Dār al-Qalam; Beirut: al-Dār al-Shāmiyya, 2009, 4th edn), 202 (*al-jamāl [huwa] al-ḥusn al-kathīr*). Compare the definition of *jamāl* in the *Lisān al-ʿarab* and the *Tāj al-ʿArūs*; the term *ḥusn* appears as a definiens in both works. See respectively Ibn Manẓūr, *The Arabic Tongue/Lisān al-ʿarab* (Beirut: Dār Ṣādir, 1956), 11:126 and Murtaḍā al-Zabīdī, *The Bridal Crown from the Gems of the Dictionary/Tāj al-ʿArūs min jawāhir al-Qāmūs*, ed. Maḥmūd Muḥammad al-Tanāḥī, rev. ʿAbd al-Salām Muḥammad Hārūn and editorial committee (Kuwait: Maṭbaʿat Ḥukūmat al-Kuwayt, 1993), 28:236.
7. Part of this awkwardness is a product of the substantive analyses of the concepts advanced by specific schools. Among Baṣran Muʿtazilites, for example, "good" (*ḥasan*) was a superordinate category that incorporated three separate qualifications: "obligatory" (*wājib*), "recommended" or "supererogatory" (*nadb* and *tafaḍḍul*), and "plain good" or "permissible" (*mubāḥ*). See briefly my *Moral Agents and their Deserts: The Character of Muʿtazilite Ethics* (Princeton, NJ: Princeton University Press, 2008), 72–73, and also 237, n. 5.
8. "Mukhtaṣar min Kitāb 'al-Akhlāq' li-Jālīnūs," in *Dirāsāt wa-nuṣūṣ fi'l-falsafa wa'l-ʿulūm ʿinda al-ʿarab*, ed. ʿAbd al-Raḥmān Badawī (Beirut: al-Muʾassasa al-ʿArabiyya liʾl-Dirāsāt waʾl-Nashr, 1981), 190–211; see, e.g., p. 199.
9. *The Arabic Version of the* Nicomachean Ethics, ed. Anna A. Akasoy and Alexander Fidora, with an introduction and annotated translation by Douglas M. Dunlop (Leiden: Brill, 2005), 163.10. Usually but not invariably; see the editors' glossary entry on *to kalon*. *Jamīl* is also the term of choice for *kalon* in the Arabic translation of the *Topics*, though the translator had to reach for more creative alternatives to convey the intricacies

of Aristotle's remarks about *kalon* as a homonymous term at 106a20–22. He opted for *naẓīf*, whose meanings include both "clean" and "beautiful." See the relevant passage in *Manṭiq Arisṭū,* ed. ʿAbd al-Raḥmān Badawī (Beirut: Dār al-Qalam; Kuwait: Wakālat al-Maṭbūʿāt, 1980), 2:511.

10. Vílchez, *Aesthetics in Arabic Thought*, 585.
11. "Mukhtaṣar," 196.
12. For all the above, see "Uthūlūjiyā Arisṭāṭālīs," in *Plotinus Apud Arabes/Aflūṭīn ʿinda al-ʿarab*, ed. ʿAbd al-Raḥmān Badawī (Cairo: Maktabat al-Nahḍa al-Miṣriyya, 1955), 56–64.
13. Adamson, *The Arabic Plotinus*, 3.2.
14. Abū Naṣr al-Fārābī, *On the Perfect State/Mabādiʾ ārāʾ ahl al-madīna al-fāḍila*, trans. Richard Walzer (Oxford: Clarendon Press, 1985), 83–85. Cf. Avicenna's remarks in *The Book of Salvation/Kitāb al-Najāt*, ed. Majid Fakhry (Beirut: Dār al-Āfāq al-Jadīda, 1985), 281–282: "the beauty and splendour of an entity consists in its being as is necessary for it to be (or: as it ought)."
15. See Avicenna, "Risāla fīʾl-ʿishq," in *Jāmiʿ al-badāʾiʿ*, ed. Muḥyī al-Dīn Ṣabrī al-Kurdī (Cairo: Maṭbaʿat al-Saʿāda, 1917), 68–91. Avicenna's concrete reference points include well-ordered sounds and tastes, though he takes a special interest in the response to the physical beauty of human beings.
16. Vílchez suggests that the term *jamīl* as applied to patience does not mean "beautiful" but "abundant," taking this to illustrate the broader point that "the lexicon related to the root *j-m-l* in the Quran can rarely be understood in a purely aesthetic sense" (*Aesthetics in Arabic Thought*, 64). He is likely basing this point on al-Rāghib's discussion (*Mufradāt*, 202: *yuqālu 'jamīl'…ʿalaʾl-takthīr*); but al-Rāghib, it is worth recalling, defines *jamāl* as an abundance specifically of *ḥusn*. The semantic scope of the latter, of course, is not confined to the aesthetic domain. More could be said about this, yet what is at the very least clear is that *ḥasan* is a term of praise; this is also the force of *jamīl* in the relevant Qurʾanic passages. Can the same be said of "abundant"?
17. See Fakhr al-Dīn al-Rāzī, *The Keys to the Unseen/Mafātīḥ al-ghayb* (Beirut: Dār al-Fikr, 1981), 18:106–107, for the above, and for a fuller explication of the criteria of the appropriate kind of patience. As al-Rāzī suggests, self-command is ultimately submission to God's command (*dhālika al-ṣabr lā yakūnu jamīlan; waʾl-ḍābiṭ anna…kulla mā kāna li-ṭalab ʿubūdiyyat Allāh taʿālā kāna ḥasanan wa-illā fa-lā*). Note the unselfconscious reduction of *jamīl* to *ḥasan* in this account.
18. *Tāj al-ʿArūs*, 28:236.
19. *Mufradāt*, 202. In his discussion of *ḥusn* (ibid, 235–236), al-Rāghib distinguishes between a type of fineness/beauty that is accessible to sight (*baṣar*) and to insight (*baṣīra*); this distinction will play an important role in al-Ghazālī's account, as we will see shortly.

Section 4

1. Good starting points for this part of al-Ghazālī's oeuvre include Sherif, *Ghazālī's Theory of Virtue*; Muhammad Abul Quasem, *The Ethics of al-Ghazālī: A Composite Ethics in Islam* (Petaling Jaya: Muhammad

Abul Quasem, 1976); and Kenneth Garden, *The First Islamic Reviver: Abū Ḥāmid al-Ghazālī and His Revival of the Religious Sciences* (Oxford: Oxford University Press, 2014). See also my "Does al-Ghazālī Have a Theory of Virtue?" for an exploration of some aspects of this intellectual "partnership" (between Sufi and philosophical ideas) in al-Ghazālī's ethics.

2. Just how to understand the relationship between these disparate ethical emphases is a topic I have explored from one direction in "Virtue and the Law in al-Ghazālī's Ethics," in *Islamic Ethics as Educational Discourse: Thought and Impact of the Classical Muslim Thinker Miskawayh*, ed. Sebastian Günther and Yassir El Jamouhi (Tübingen: Mohr Siebeck, 2021).
3. *Iḥyāʾ*, 8:1434.
4. Ibid.
5. *Iḥyāʾ*, 1:89.
6. This of course presupposes that the connection between virtue and beauty may not be transparent to the inquirer. The possibility of this cognitive shortfall is consistent with al-Ghazālī's discussion elsewhere, as we will see.
7. I have discussed this concern further in relation to al-Ghazālī's and other intellectuals' articulation of the virtues of magnanimity and greatness of spirit in *Virtues of Greatness in the Arabic Tradition* (Oxford: Oxford University Press, 2019); see especially 31–34 and 144 ff. Cf. Panos Paris' comment on this point in "Moral Beauty and Education," *Journal of Moral Education* 48 (2019), 406–407.
8. The normative accent in the quoted remark is in fact partly a construct of the context, as al-Ghazālī is distinguishing between different types of motivation for the pursuit of intellectual understanding, and urging this motivation over a less salutary type directed to external goods such as honour and wealth.
9. This idea finds its clearest expression in *The Most Exalted Aim in Expounding God's Beautiful Names*/*Al-Maqṣad al-asnā fī sharḥ maʿānī asmāʾ Allāh al-ḥusnā*, ed. Fadlou A. Shehadi (Beirut: Dar El-Machreq, 1971), 126–127.
10. *Iḥyāʾ*, 13:2335 (*innamā al-maḥmūdu fī nafsihi…kullu mā yajūzu an yūṣafa Allāhu taʿālā bihi, wa-mā lā yajūzu…fa-laysa bi-kamālin fī dhātihi*). Though it is one of the main thrusts of the *Maqṣad* to add a twist to this view: what is a virtue in God will typically have to be exemplified in a rather different sense by human beings.
11. *Maqṣad*, 44.
12. This may of course seem question-begging, and not to fully address the depth of the concern framed above. See the concluding section for an additional set of remarks that place this point in context.
13. Love of an object, after all, depends on awareness of that object, as al-Ghazālī points out in *On Love* (*Iḥyāʾ*, 14:2574). This is also a key theme of the discussion in *Maqṣad*; see especially 42 ff.
14. *Iḥyāʾ*, 14:2574. Once again this echoes ideas expressed by the *falāsifa*; compare e.g. the discussion in Avicenna, *Najāt*, 282.
15. There is some textual prevarication as to whether this sense consists in the heart or is located in the heart: *Iḥyāʾ*, 14:2575.
16. Ibid.

17. Al-Ghazālī seems to present different drafts of this taxonomy as his discussion progresses; I rely on the overview provided at ibid, 2581.
18. It may be noted that many of these objects of attachment correspond to the objectives of the Law (*maqāṣid al-sharīʿa*) as tabulated by legal theorists, including al-Ghazālī himself. Al-Ghazālī clearly tags these objects as egoistic—a point that can be placed in conversation with his account of the limitations of jurisprudential science in book 1 of the *Revival*.
19. There is a related paradox, as we will see shortly, as to why beneficence 2 is not filed under intrinsic love. Further, logically speaking, love of self is also a form of intrinsic love. I am not the first to notice certain wrinkles in al-Ghazālī's presentation, or to attempt to iron them out; from a different direction, see e.g. Abrahamov, *Divine Love*, 51, and Van Den Bergh, "The 'Love of God'," 314.
20. Al-Ghazālī unfolds this argument in concentration at *Iḥyāʾ*, 14:2581–2592.
21. This is the sort he describes as the "profound true love that can be trusted to endure" at ibid, 2577.
22. Ibid.
23. In combination, more broadly, with the ancient tendency to make the ethical focus the quality of our lives as a whole. Good starting points for thinking through these questions are Julia Annas, *The Morality of Happiness* (Oxford: Oxford University Press, 1993), Chapter 2.7; idem, *Intelligent Virtue* (Oxford: Oxford University Press, 2011), 152–163; and more briefly with reference to Aristotle, Terence H. Irwin, *The Development of Ethics*, vol. 1: *From Socrates to the Reformation* (Oxford: Oxford University Press, 2007), §114.
24. *Iḥyāʾ*, 14:2577–2578.
25. Ibid, 2578.
26. Scruton, *Art and Imagination: A Study in the Philosophy of Mind* (South Bend, IN: St Augustine's Press, 1998), 148. This view is certainly not without its critics; see, for example, briefly, Gaut, *Art, Emotion and Ethics*, Chapter 2.1. This view of aesthetic experience is often taken to supply important grounds for distinguishing between art and pornography. Al-Ghazālī himself does not focus on the outward human form as an aesthetic object, so does not confront the special challenges this poses. This contrasts interestingly with Avicenna, who takes pains to distinguish between two different modes of responding to (of loving) physical human beauty, one associated with our appetitive animal nature and the other with our intellectual nature. See "Risāla fiʾl-ʿishq," 80–83.
27. *The World as Will and Representation*, 1:197. The therapeutic effect of exposure to nature is of course also widely discussed outside philosophical circles these days.
28. See the discussion in Nick Zangwill, *The Metaphysics of Beauty* (Ithaca, NY; London: Cornell University Press, 2001), Chapter 8; 127 quoted.
29. See text to notes 4 and 5, Section 1.
30. Or "course of life"; the term can also refer to a record or account of this course (*vita*), as will emerge further on.
31. *Iḥyāʾ*, 14:2578–2579.
32. *Maqṣad*, 126.
33. An alternative translation is possible: "making the truthful Abū Bakr truthful."

34. *Iḥyāʾ*, 14:2579–2580.
35. See, respectively, *Iḥyāʾ*, 14:2578, and *Maqṣad*, 126.
36. "Typically," though al-Ghazālī's terminology raises difficult questions which complicate this statement. For a survey of scholarly perspectives on the topic and an attempt to resolve these questions, see my "Does al-Ghazālī Have a Theory of Virtue?" And see *Iḥyāʾ*, 12:2171 for the passage cited. Insofar as the love of virtuous exemplars incorporates an express judgement of value, al-Ghazālī's understanding aligns itself closely with some of the most prominent recent cognitivist accounts of emotions. See e.g. Martha C. Nussbaum, *Upheavals of Thought: The Intelligence of Emotions* (Cambridge; New York: Cambridge University Press, 2001), for a notable account along these lines intended to contest the conception of emotions as irrational or brute.
37. For a well-known statement of this "paradox," see Colin Radford, "How Can We Be Moved by the Fate of Anna Karenina?" *Proceedings of the Aristotelian Society, Supplementary Volumes* 49 (1975), 67–80. As Derek Matravers reformulates the point (without endorsing it), it is the problem posed by the fact that "[a]mongst the causes of an emotion felt towards p, it is necessary that there be a belief that p is actual, or likely to be actual, or has been actual"—a condition that our emotional response to fictional characters and events appears to violate. See his *Fiction and Narrative* (Oxford: Oxford University Press, 2014), 103, and generally Chapter 8 for critical discussion.
38. For discussion, see Anne-Marie Schimmel, *And Mohammed Is His Messenger: The Veneration of the Prophet in Islamic Piety* (Chapel Hill, NC; London: University of North Carolina Press, 1985), Chapter 2. One of the best-known exemplars of this genre, by the Mālikite jurist and traditionist Qāḍī ʿIyāḍ (d. 1149), dwells at some length on the necessity of loving the Prophet. See al-Qāḍī ʿIyāḍ, *The Curative Knowledge of the Claims of the Chosen Prophet/al-Shifāʾ bi-taʿrīf ḥuqūq al-muṣṭafā*, ed. ʿAlī Muḥammad al-Bajāwī (Beirut: Dār al-Kitāb al-ʿArabī, 1984), 2:563ff. (Parts of this discussion in fact echo al-Ghazālī's account of love in the *Revival* so closely they can only be thought of as a direct adaptation of it; see especially 2:579–581.) At the same time, the author clearly presupposes the existence of such attitudes in his reader and seems to think of his persuasive aim not so much to generate them *ab ovo* as to deepen and develop them, as the opening lines of 1:77 suggest ("You who love this noble Prophet … and who are seeking to go beyond generalities to grasp the particulars of his sublime status …").
39. *Iḥyāʾ*, 14:2580.
40. Ibid.
41. On one level, al-Ghazālī theorises the virtues as simply different ways of mastering the bodily appetites and attachments to worldly goods. This is reflected in his description of the virtues and the vices as, respectively, "dispositions of domination" (*hayʾāt istilāʾiyya*) and "dispositions of subservience" (*hayʾāt inqiyādiyya*)—that is, relative to the appetites. *The Scale of Action/Mīzān al-ʿamal*, ed. Sulaymān Dunyā (Cairo: Dār al-Maʿārif, 1964), 204.
42. A more literal translation: "in describing him as courageous, generous," etc.

43. *Iḥyāʾ*, 14:2580.
44. Ibid, cf. 2585.
45. Kukkonen, "The Good, the Beautiful," 87.
46. Al-Ghazālī has rather more to say on this topic in an earlier book of the *Revival*, namely *On Intimacy, Brotherhood and Companionship*, where he offers a related but not identical taxonomy of the different types of love that human beings may attract (*Iḥyāʾ*, 5:931). The first type, intrinsic love, anticipates the discussion of beauty in *On Love* (ibid, 931–934). Interestingly, in one passage al-Ghazālī appears to discount this as a form of love "based [merely] on natural disposition and psychic appetite" (*ḥubb biʾl-ṭabʿ wa-shahwat al-nafs*) which even non-believers may experience. It is unclear from the context, however, whether this evaluation concerns only the response to physical beauty (mentioned in the vicinity of this remark) or also to moral beauty, thus declaring the human love based on the latter inferior to the spiritual companionship that al-Ghazālī goes on to describe as "love for and in God" (*ḥubb liʾl-Lāh wa-fiʾl-Lāh*), in which love of other human beings derives from the relation they bear to God as the primary object of love. If the latter, it would suggest that the intrinsic love of moral beauty is deficient insofar as it makes no reference to God, and that the best way of loving virtue is not for its own sake (under its aspect as beautiful) but for the sake of God (under its aspect as loved by God). Cf. e.g. the phrasing at ibid, 938: *athmara ḥubba kulli man fīhi ṣifa murḍiya ʿinda Allāhi min khuluq ḥasan*, though this remark admits of more than one reading. This focus—on evaluative objects as valued or disvalued *qua* loved or hated by God—also dominates the perspective of the book *On Meditation*, though mainly apropos action. Taken as an account of the best type of moral motivation (we should love the virtues because God loves them), my sense is that this interpretation can be harmonised with al-Ghazālī's overall approach. Taken as an account of moral ontology (they *are* in fact virtues because God loves them), it seems more problematic, and it would have important implications for the present discussion, especially for the issues raised in the next section; but the evidence for it does not seem decisive.
47. Wittgenstein, "Philosophy of Psychology—A Fragment, §25," in *Philosophical Investigations,* ed. Peter M. S. Hacker and Joachim Schulte, trans. G. E. M. Anscombe, Peter M. S. Hacker, and Joachim Schulte (Chichester: Wiley-Blackwell, 2009, 4th rev. edn).
48. Cf. George Orwell's well-known epigram, as I read it: "At 50, everyone has the face he deserves."
49. Ian James Kidd, "Admiration, Attraction and the Aesthetics of Exemplarity," *Journal of Moral Education* 48 (2019), 373–374. See also his "Beauty, Virtue, and Religious Exemplars," *Religious Studies* 53 (2017), 171–181. His account in turn builds on David E. Cooper's discussion, e.g. in his "Beautiful People, Beautiful Things," *British Journal of Aesthetics* 48 (2008), 247–260, in the context of a larger and rather radical conception of beauty. Kidd does not directly address the limitations of this view taken as a general account of the aesthetic experience of character, given that it is restricted to exemplars with whom one has "personal" rather than "testimonial" or "narrative" encounters, on his terms ("Admiration, Attraction," 370–371).
50. *Mīzān*, 299.

51. Nietzsche, *Twilight of the Idols* and *the Anti-Christ*, trans. R. J. Hollingdale (London: Penguin, 1990), 40.
52. This is the line suggested by Avicenna, for example, in "Risāla fiʾl-ʿishq," 81–82. And see Rosenthal, "On Art and Aesthetics," for some references to the idea in wisdom literature, with an emphasis on its contestation.
53. *Mīzān*, 300. Al-Ghazālī's specification of beauty further down (300–301) introduces an extra layer of complexity, which I won't try to grapple with here.
54. See, respectively, Sara B. Algoe and Jonathan Haidt, "Witnessing Excellence in Action: The 'Other-Praising' Emotions of Elevation, Gratitude, and Admiration," *Journal of Positive Psychology* 4 (2009), 105–127; Jonathan Haidt, "Elevation and the Positive Psychology of Morality," in *Flourishing: Positive Psychology and the Life Well-Lived*, ed. Corey L. M. Keyes and Jonathan Haidt (Washington, DC: American Psychological Association, 2003), 275–280; Kristján Kristjánsson, "Emotions Targeting Moral Exemplarity: Making Sense of the Logical Geography of Admiration, Emulation and Elevation," *Theory and Research in Education* 15 (2017), 20–37; Panos Paris, "The Empirical Case for Moral Beauty," *Australasian Journal of Philosophy* 96 (2018), 642–656.
55. Compare Ibn Taymiyya's understanding of human nature as discussed in my *Ibn Taymiyya's Theological Ethics* (New York: Oxford University Press, 2016), Chapter 2, esp. 89–90. Taken together, in fact, all the above suggests that we must regard al-Ghazālī as one of the most important influences on the special brand of moral sentimentalism developed by Ibn Taymiyya, which likewise drew the moral into close connection with the aesthetic and was articulated as a form of ethical naturalism. For further comment on al-Ghazālī's conception of *fiṭra* from a different direction, see Frank Griffel, "Al-Ghazālī's Use of "Original Human Disposition" (*Fiṭra*) and Its Background in the Teachings of al-Fārābī and Avicenna," *Muslim World* 102 (2012), 1–32.
56. An alternative or complementary explanation is that the *Revival* is not the type of work in which al-Ghazālī would confront such challenges; see the discussion in Section 6.
57. On this point, see, briefly, my "Does al-Ghazālī Have a Theory of Virtue?" As al-Ghazālī puts the point more generally in *Iḥyāʾ*, 13:2340, using *faḍīla* in the sense of "value": "the value of any given thing depends on its utility for conducing to the happiness that consists in encountering God" (*inna faḍīlat al-shayʾ bi-qadr ghināʾihi fiʾl-ifḍāʾ ilā saʿādat liqāʾ Allāh*). The question how these two explanatory views relate could take interesting discussion.

Section 5

1. Put very briefly: his account of God's virtues is overwhelmingly negative and rests on an analytical reduction of the virtues (in their entire colourful rainbow) to two features, knowledge and power. Both moves would seem to introduce a gulf between our reaction to God and our ordinary reactions to human beauty of character.
2. I have especially in mind Paris, "On Form."
3. "Mukhtaṣar," 195 ff; 199: *mayl al-nās ilaʾl-jamīl biʾl-ṭabʿ kabīr.*

4. See Rosenthal, "On Art and Aesthetics."
5. Arent J. Wensinck's view (*La Pensée de Ghazzālī* [Paris: Adrien-Maisonneuve, 1940], 24ff) is approvingly echoed by Richard Walzer in *The Perfect State*, 350–351; Van den Bergh makes the same assumption, though apparently more from prejudice than from evidence, in his rather patronising discussion in "The 'Love of God'." Vílchez also views al-Ghazālī's discussion as derivative (*Aesthetics in Arabic Thought*, 737ff) though his focus is not exclusively on philosophical influences.
6. "On Art and Aesthetics," 12.
7. *Mufradāt*, 202 and 235–236, as quoted earlier.
8. For this point, and for al-Rāghib's influence on al-Ghazālī, see Wilferd Madelung, "Ar-Rāġib al-Iṣfahānī und die Ethik al-Ġazālīs," in *Islamwissenschaftliche Abhandlungen Fritz Meier zum sechzigsten Geburtstag*, ed. Richard Gramlich (Steiner: Wiesbaden, 1974), 152–163; Hans Daiber, "Griechische Ethik in islamischem Gewande: Das Beispiel von Rāġib al-Iṣfahānī (11. Jh.)," in *Historia Philosophiae Medii Aevi: Studien zur Geschichte der Philosophie des Mittelalters*, ed. Burkhard Mojsisch and Olaf Pluta (Amsterdam; Philadelphia: Grüner, 1991), 1:181–192; Jules Janssens, "Al-Ghazālī's *Mīzān al-ʿAmal*: An Ethical Summa Based on Ibn Sīnā and al-Rāghib al-Iṣfahānī," in *Islamic Thought in the Middle Ages: Studies in Text, Transmission and Translation in Honour of Hans Daiber*, ed. Anna Akasoy and Wim Raven (Leiden: Brill, 2008), 123–137; and Yasien Mohamed in several pieces, including "The Ethical Philosophy of al-Rāghib al-Iṣfahānī," *Journal of Islamic Studies* 6 (1995), 51–75, and "The Ethics of Education: al-Iṣfahānī's *al-Dharīʿa* as a Source of Inspiration for al-Ghazālī's *Mīzān al-ʿAmal*," *Muslim World* 101 (2011), 633–657.
9. This would be the case even if we took the (contestable) view that Islamic ethics just *is* Islamic law.
10. *The Quintessence of the Principles of Law/Al-Mustaṣfā min ʿilm al-uṣūl* (Būlāq: al-Maṭbaʿa al-Amīriyya, 1322 [1904]), 1:56, in the context of a threefold classification of the meanings of the term *ḥasan*. Cf. Vasalou, *Ibn Taymiyya's Theological Ethics*, 26–27.
11. *Moderation in Belief/Al-Iqtiṣād fiʾl-iʿtiqād*, ed. Ibrahim Agâh Çubukçu and Hüseyin Atay (Ankara: Nur Matbaasi, 1962), 190.
12. For more detail on this aspect of Ashʿarite ethical thinking, and on al-Ghazālī's more specific contribution, see my *Ibn Taymiyya's Theological Ethics*, Chapter 3.
13. *Mustaṣfā*, 1:61; cf. *Ibn Taymiyya's Theological Ethics*, 38–39.
14. *Iḥyāʾ*, 14:2575, as quoted earlier. Cf. the apposition of reason and nature two lines down ("the inclination of sound nature and right reason," *mayl al-ṭabʿ al-salīm waʾl-ʿaql al-ṣaḥīḥ*).
15. For more on the Muʿtazilite use of such empirical claims and on al-Ghazālī's and his fellow-Ashʿarites' critique, see my *Ibn Taymiyya's Theological Ethics*, 38–39, 110–113.
16. It's not incidental to note that the emphasis on the Prophet's extensive beneficence shapes the corresponding discussion in al-Qāḍī ʿIyāḍ's *al-Shifāʾ bi-taʿrīf ḥuqūq al-muṣṭafā* (2:579–581) which, as suggested above, reads like a direct adaptation of the *Revival*.
17. See *Iḥyāʾ*, 10:1837–1838, and my *Virtues of Greatness*, 35–37, for some context and discussion.

18. For a fuller discussion of this point, see my "Virtue and the Law in al-Ghazālī's Ethics."
19. *Iḥyāʾ*, 14:2586.
20. *Treatise of Human Nature*, 477.
21. "Intrinsic value"? This characterisation might seem open to question given what was said earlier concerning al-Ghazālī's higher-level views about virtue: a character trait is a virtue if it is a virtue in God, and for moral virtues, if it is instrumental to the realisation of our intellectual potentialities. Both of these views entail that the value of the virtues exemplified by human beings is in fact relative on either one or both of those levels. This description would appear to align the viewpoint of the *Revival* rather more closely with the viewpoint of al-Ghazālī's theological and legal works. It would also suggest that ordinary judgements on the virtues may be mistaken insofar as they take the virtues to be intrinsically valuable (presumably al-Ghazālī would not consider that when ordinary people perceive certain kinds of character as beautiful, their judgements are grounded in an awareness, however inarticulate, of these higher-level facts about what makes a character trait a virtue). There would then be an ostensible analogy with the viewpoint expressed in al-Ghazālī's theological and legal works (to be outlined shortly in the main text) with reference to ordinary judgements on certain classes of actions. Just as we may think certain actions, such as lying, are intrinsically/absolutely bad because we don't grasp the psychological foundations of our evaluative responses (namely, our egoistic drives), we may think certain traits are intrinsically good because we don't grasp the metaphysical foundations of the right evaluative responses (and in both cases, mistakes on this meta-ethical level translate into mistakes in the evaluation of substantive actions and traits). Yet the analogy is ultimately not the strongest, as closer scrutiny of this last framing would already show. In the main text, I will suggest some additional reasons why I am sceptical of this attempt to reconcile the two viewpoints (taking the al-Ghazālī of the *Revival* to be deliberately limiting himself to epistemically dubious moral *endoxa*), but I am aware the issue could take far more discussion and disentangling.
22. *Mustaṣfā*, 1:58; though it is worth noting that the Muʿtazilites, like the al-Ghazālī of the *Mustaṣfā*, viewed acts, not states of character, as the main object of moral concern.
23. Ibid, 1:56; cf. *Iqtiṣād*, 164. Compare briefly, apropos Ibn Taymiyya's related move, Vasalou, *Ibn Taymiyya's Theological Ethics*, 42–43.
24. See Abū Ḥayyān al-Tawḥīdī and Abū ʿAlī Miskawayh, *The Philosopher Responds: An Intellectual Correspondence From the Tenth Century*, ed. Bilal Orfali and Maurice A. Pomerantz, trans. Sophia Vasalou and James E. Montgomery (New York: New York University Press, 2019), 1:212–219. Cf. Vílchez, *Aesthetics in Arabic Thought*, 210–212.
25. Though even al-Ghazālī marks a certain sort of distinction in the *Moderation* when he refers to the "aesthetic" application of *ḥasan* as "sensory" or "physical" (*al-ḥusn al-maḥsūs*). *Iqtiṣād*, 164.
26. ʿAbd al-Jabbār, *The Sufficiency in God's Unity and Justice/al-Mughnī fī abwāb al-tawḥīd waʾl-ʿadl*, vol. 6/1: *al-Taʿdīl waʾl-tajwīr*, ed. Aḥmad Fuʾād al-Ahwānī (Cairo: al-Muʾassasa al-Miṣriyya al-ʿĀmma liʾl-Taʾlīf waʾl-Tarjama waʾl-Ṭibāʿa waʾl-Nashr, 1962), 19–21. As ʿAbd al-Jabbār

makes clear, from his perspective it is of secondary importance whether the analysis of the terms he provides (*ḥusn, qubḥ*, etc.) constitutes an accurate descriptive account of linguistic usage, as against of intelligible reality (the level of *maʿnan*); yet he nevertheless maintains that his analysis does represent such an account. See especially the remark at ibid, 25. For further comment on ʿAbd al-Jabbār's definition of evil, including his attempt to differentiate between ethical and aesthetic judgements, see George F. Hourani, *Islamic Rationalism: The Ethics of ʿAbd al-Jabbār* (Oxford: Clarendon Press, 1971), Chapter 4, especially 49–55. Interestingly, Hourani assumes the *aesthetic* meaning was primary and was transferred to ethical qualities at a secondary stage.

27. *Taʿdīl*, 25. Cf. Mānkdīm Shashdīw's distinction between what is bad/ugly "from the perspective of look and appearance" (*min jihat al-marʾā waʾl-manẓar*) and "from the perspective of reason and wisdom" (*min jihat al-ʿaql waʾl-ḥikma*) in *[Taʿlīq] Sharḥ al-Uṣūl al-khamsa*, ed. ʿAbd al-Karīm ʿUthmān (Cairo: Maktabat Wahba, 1965), 505–506.

Section 6

1. For more context on this point, see my "Ethics as Medicine: Moral Therapy, Expertise, and Practical Reasoning in al-Ghazālī's Ethics," *Archiv für Geschichte der Philosophie* (2021). https://doi.org/10.1515/agph-2020-5006
2. For the above, see W. Montgomery Watt, "Al-Ghazālī," in *Encyclopaedia of Islam, Second Edition*, ed. P. Bearman, Th. Bianquis, C.E. Bosworth, E. van Donzel, and W.P. Heinrichs. Consulted online on 23 August 2020: http://dx.doi.org/10.1163/1573-3912_islam_COM_0233. Cf. the remarks in Watt, *Muslim Intellectual: A Study of al-Ghazālī* (Edinburgh: Edinburgh University Press, 1963), 67–68. The *Deliverer*'s view of philosophical ethics that Watt references is arguably more irenic than he suggests. For some discussion, see Vasalou, *Virtues of Greatness*, 53–54, in the context of trying to resolve another apparent conflict in al-Ghazālī's expressed positions; Sherif, *Ghazālī's Theory of Virtue*, 17–18; and more extensively, Taneli Kukkonen, "Al-Ghazālī on the Origins of Ethics," *Numen* 63 (2016), 271–298. Another strategy for negotiating observed conflicts is to take them as grounds for reappraising the authenticity of certain of al-Ghazālī's works, or certain parts of these works. This strategy was also adopted by Watt apropos the *Mīzān* in "The Authenticity of the Works Attributed to al-Ghazālī," *Journal of the Royal Asiatic Society of Great Britain and Ireland* 1/2 (1952), 38–40.
3. See, e.g., Frank Griffel, *Al-Ghazālī's Philosophical Theology* (New York: Oxford University Press, 2009), especially the positioning statement on p. 43. The point has been made with reference to al-Ghazālī's ethics more specifically by Garden in *The First Islamic Reviver*; cf. his "Revisiting al-Ghazālī's Crisis Through his *Scale for Action* (*Mizān al-ʿAmal*)," in *Islam and Rationality: The Impact of al-Ghazālī*, vol. 1, ed. Georges Tamer (Leiden: Brill, 2015), 207–228. This is also Sherif's implicit assumption in *Ghazālī's Theory of Virtue*.
4. See George F. Hourani, "A Revised Chronology of Ghazālī's Writings," *Journal of the American Oriental Society* 104 (1984), 289–302.

5. Timothy J. Gianotti, *Al-Ghazālī's Unspeakable Doctrine of the Soul: Unveiling the Esoteric Psychology and Eschatology of the* Iḥyāʾ (Leiden: Brill, 2001).
6. This styling of the question itself represents a fine instance of dust-throwing given that little in the book evokes the Ashʿarite perspective and much evokes the philosophical one, which al-Ghazālī does not even entertain as a possible self-identification.
7. *Mīzān*, 405–409.
8. Gianotti, *Al-Ghazālī's Unspeakable Doctrine*, 6.
9. Richard M. Frank, *Al-Ghazālī and the Ashʿarite School* (Durham, NC; London: Duke University Press, 1994), 86, 87. I should note that this basic methodological convergence leaves ample room for other disagreements between Gianotti and Frank.
10. *Iḥyāʾ*, 1:168; and see generally the discussion 163–171. Cf. Gianotti, *Al-Ghazālī's Unspeakable Doctrine*, 45–50; Frank, *Al-Ghazālī and the Ashʿarite School*, Chapter 2 and passim.
11. Frank, *Al-Ghazālī and the Ashʿarite School*, 75. In terms of the three-tiered scheme of the *Scale* (discussed in ibid, 96–97), Frank reads the *Moderation* as belonging either to the first or the second tier (representing al-Ghazālī's doctrine for scholastic disputation or public teaching); ibid, 99.
12. Al-Ghazālī, to be sure, distinguishes between different levels of assent to, and understanding of, the truth; but he remains adamant that these different levels—exterior and interior, overt and covert (*ẓāhir/bāṭin, ʿalin/sirr, jaliyy/khafiyy*)—cannot be in conflict. See the discussion in *Iḥyāʾ*, 1:171–180. As far as I can see, the fivefold taxonomy of esoteric truths he provides in this context also furnishes no analytical tools that would help us account for the apparent conflict we are considering, though that could take longer discussion.
13. For some discussion of this point, see my *Moral Agents and their Deserts*, Chapter 2.
14. Besides the point outlined next, there is a further consideration, which introduces too many complexities to mention in the main text. The epistemic demotion of al-Ghazālī's theological works has usually been proposed in the context of—and motivated by—a perceived conflict between his expressed views, where his other views are aligned with the intellectual paradigm of the philosophers (notably Avicenna). Yet whatever conflicts might be perceived in other areas, in the specific topic of metaethics Ashʿarite theology had entered into a deep partnership with Avicennan ideas, harnessing Avicenna's account of widely accepted propositions or *endoxa* (*mashhūrāt*) to serve the campaign against the Muʿtazilite claim that moral qualities are objective and moral propositions are known by reason. (For more on this, see my *Ibn Taymiyya's Theological Ethics*, esp. 58–65, 112–113; for a number of reasons, I am unconvinced by Frank's attempt to bring out the latent conflict of al-Ghazālī's account of ethics in the *Moderation* with traditional Ashʿarite doctrine in *Al-Ghazālī and the Ashʿarite School*, 32–36.) In this case, therefore, the motivation for this type of hermeneutic appears to be lacking. At the same time, this will seem curious given the influence of philosophical texts in shaping the very *rationalist-objectivist* perspective

of al-Ghazālī's virtue-centred works, which I have been describing as conflicting with that of his *kalām* works. Buried here might be the seed of some yet-unimagined "supercharged" interpretation.

15. Gianotti, *Al-Ghazālī's Unspeakable Doctrine*, 32.
16. Kukkonen, "The Good, the Beautiful," 99–100.
17. *Iḥyāʾ*, 8:1344, using the term *qalb*. The former knowledge belongs to the science of disclosure, *ʿilm al-mukāshafa* (*Iḥyāʾ*, 1:91). Cf. *Iḥyāʾ*, 8:1406, responding to a request that he clarify whether it is one devil or many discrete ones that collude to entice one to discrete kinds of sin.
18. *Mustaṣfā*, 1:58. Al-Ghazālī names a second possible cause or foundation, namely adherence to religious belief (*al-tadayyun biʾl-sharāʾiʿ*); but at least at the stage of initial motivation, the two coincide.
19. See note 14 (this section) and references there. The term "veneer theory" is associated with the Dutch primatologist Frans de Waal in his writings on morality.
20. I'm slightly simplifying, and there's also a more complex story to be told concerning Ibn Taymiyya's relation to Ashʿarism, as I've argued in *Ibn Taymiyya's Theological Ethics*, especially Chapter 3.
21. Griffel, *Al-Ghazālī's Philosophical Theology*, 286. While I wholeheartedly agree with this sentiment, I am far less convinced of the interpretation of the *Scale* to which Griffel conjoins it; see ibid, 359, n. 45.
22. The quoted remark is from ibid, 278. Griffel's emphasis on the disjunction between the domains of metaphysical explanation and practical action (where "commonly held assumptions" about causality, p. 285, may be allowed to operate unchecked) may evoke al-Ghazālī's earlier distinction between commonly held assumptions about ethics (*mashhūrāt*) and their deeper foundations (*mustanad*). Might it thus be possible to redeploy Griffel's explanation to the latter case and use it to unlock its puzzle? The analogy seems suggestive, but closer consideration would reveal too many differences between the two cases to make it fruitful.
23. Abuʾl-Ḥasan al-Ashʿarī, *Spotlights on the Confrontation of Deviance and Innovation/Kitāb al-Lumaʿ fiʾl-radd ʿalā ahl al-zaygh waʾl-bidaʿ*, ed. Ḥammūda Ghurāba (Cairo: Maṭbaʿat Miṣr, 1955), 117.
24. This is not meant to overlook the more expansive evaluative spectrum to be found in both theological and legal works, such as the concept of supererogation (*tafaḍḍul*) in Muʿtazilite ethics, or the concept of discouraged (*makrūh*) and recommended (*mustaḥabb*) actions in the context of law. The latter evaluations, in particular, have sometimes been described as testaments to the aspirational aspect of the *sharīʿa*, where its concern shades out of the legal and into the ethical and it seeks to promote, in Mohammad Hashim Kamali's words, "moral virtues and the attainment of excellence in conduct" (*Shari'ah Law: An Introduction* [Oxford: Oneworld, 2008], 18).
25. Henry Sidgwick, *The Methods of Ethics* (Indianapolis, IN: Hackett, 1981, 7th edn), 105.
26. Kosman, "Beauty and the Good," 356.
27. Carl Ernst's implicit distinction between two different ways of regarding the Prophet—as an object of obedience, and as an object of attraction, the latter particularly pronounced in Sufi literature—seems especially suggestive in pointing to this diremption of paradigms, one defined by obedience and

a morality of law-like command, the other by admiration and a morality of beautiful example. See his "Muḥammad as the Pole of Existence," in *The Cambridge Companion to Muḥammad*, ed. Jonathan E. Brockopp (Cambridge: Cambridge University Press, 2010), esp. 129–132, for discussion. The contrast, again, cannot be drawn too sharply. *Inter alia*, Sufis typically emphasised the importance of adherence to the *sharīʿa* taken as a system of rules. And the Prophet's personal example also has legislative force and serves as the source of law-like commands. Unsurprisingly, these two paradigms coexist in important representatives of the textual tradition; al-Qāḍī ʿIyāḍ's *al-Shifāʾ bi-taʿrīf ḥuqūq al-muṣṭafā* is again a good example, the emphasis on the human obligation of loving the Prophet sharing its space in the book with the emphasis on the obligation of obeying him.

28. This concern registers strongly in the *Maqṣad*, which develops the idea of imitating God's attributes (or acquiring His beautiful names) against a sharp distinction between the sense in which these attributes are predicated of God and the sense in which they apply to and can be realised by human beings. This points to a fundamental tension in the *Maqṣad* about how to reconcile God's immanence and transcendence, or his comparability and incomparability. For a deeper meditation on this theme, see Yousef Casewit, "Al-Ghazālī's Virtue Ethical Theory of the Divine Names: The Theological Underpinnings of the Doctrine of *Takhalluq* in *al-Maqṣad al-Asnā*," *Journal of Islamic Ethics* 4 (2020), 155–200.
29. See my brief remarks in *Ibn Taymiyya's Theological Ethics*, 47–48. Though Ibn Taymiyya, for his part, focuses on action rather than states of character in developing his view; and the wheels it greases more immediately, as I suggest, concern Ibn Taymiyya's assertion of the natural human love for the good.
30. See, for example, the discussion in *Iqtiṣād*, 192–195; cf. *Ibn Taymiyya's Theological Ethics*, 156–157 and references there.
31. *Iḥyāʾ*, 8:1426. Al-Ghazālī's view of this conduciveness, it is true, builds on a claim about the serviceability of moral to intellectual virtue (hence loving cognition of God) that he would appear to have absorbed from the Greek philosophical tradition, where it was supposedly developed without access to religious scripture. Perhaps the account he provides in the *Deliverer*, where he reverses the explanatory order by claiming it was the philosophers who derived their ethical insights from mystics and religious men (*The Deliverer From Error/Al-Munqidh min al-ḍalāl*, ed. Jamīl Ṣalībā and Kāmil ʿAyyād [Beirut: Dār al-Andalus, 1967], 86), should here be seeing as supplying the missing piece and plugging the remaining gap.
32. This point is central, for example, to the account of admiration on which Linda T. Zagzebski builds her moral theory in *Exemplarist Moral Theory* (New York: Oxford University Press, 2017), though she approaches the idea of "cognitive processing" on rather more specific terms. Compare Kristján Kristjánsson's view as discussed in Sophia Vasalou, "Admiration, Emulation, and the Description of Character," *Journal of Aesthetic Education* 54 (2020), 47–69.
33. "At least in part," because al-Ghazālī holds that possession of the virtues is also a means to this-worldly happiness, its value thus in principle transparent even within a naturalistic framework free from such metaphysical baggage. See *Mīzān*, 190–193.

Section 7

1. Kosman, "Beauty and the Good," 353. Cf. Charles Kahn: besides its aesthetic overtones, the pair *kalon-aischron* "refers primarily to the realm of honour and respect, social approval and disapproval" ("Pre-Platonic Ethics," *Ethics—Companions to Ancient Thought: 4*, ed. Stephen Everson [Cambridge: Cambridge University Press, 1998], 27).
2. For all the above, see Kosman, "Beauty and the Good," 353–355.
3. Bernard Williams, *Shame and Necessity* (Berkeley, LA: University of California Press, 1993), 78 and 82; the other may not be a particular individual or the representative of a particular social group but instead identified in ethical terms as an idealised and generalised observer "whose reactions I would respect" (ibid, 81–84). Cf. Peter Hacker: "the *conceptual iconography* of feeling ashamed is *the eye of others*" ("Shame, Embarrassment, and Guilt," *Midwest Studies in Philosophy* 41 [2017], 219).
4. Hacker, "Shame, Embarrassment," 203, rehearsing an understanding of the distinction between shame and guilt cultures popularised by the anthropologist Ruth Benedict.
5. This is a theme of my *Virtues of Greatness*, which casts a spotlight on the preservation and renegotiation of a specific set of pre-Islamic Arab values, as represented by the heroic virtue of greatness of spirit (*ʕiẓam/ buʕd al-himma*). See especially 108ff.
6. Books 28 and 29 of the *Revival*: *On the Condemnation of Status and Dissimulation*, and *On the Condemnation of Pride and Conceit.*
7. Hacker, "Shame, Embarrassment," 202.
8. Friedrich Nietzsche, "On the Uses and Disadvantages of History for Life," *Untimely Meditations*, ed. Daniel Breazeale, trans. R. J. Hollingdale (Cambridge: Cambridge University Press, 1997), 67, 68.

Bibliography

ʿAbd al-Jabbār ibn Aḥmad al-Asadābādī. *The Sufficiency in God's Unity and Justice/al-Mughnī fī abwāb al-tawḥīd wa'l-ʿadl*, vol. 6/1: *al-Taʿdīl wa'l-tajwīr*, edited by Aḥmad Fuʾād al-Ahwānī. Cairo: al-Muʾassasa al-Miṣriyya al-ʿĀmma liʾl-Taʾlīf waʾl-Tarjama waʾl-Ṭibāʿa waʾl-Nashr, 1962.

Abrahamov, Binyamin. *Divine Love in Islamic Mysticism: The Teachings of Al-Ghazâlî and Al-Dabbâgh*. London; New York: Routledge, 2003.

———. "Al-Ghazālī and the Rationalization of Sufism." In *Islam and Rationality: The Impact of al-Ghazālī*, vol. 1, edited by Georges Tamer, 35–48. Leiden: Brill, 2015.

Abul Quasem, Muhammad. *The Ethics of al-Ghazālī: A Composite Ethics in Islam*. Petaling Jaya: Muhammad Abul Quasem, 1976.

Adamson, Peter. *The Arabic Plotinus: A Study of the Theology of Aristotle*. London: Duckworth, 2002.

Aersten, Jan A. *Medieval Philosophy and the Transcendentals: The Case of Thomas Aquinas*. Leiden: E.J. Brill, 1996.

Algoe, Sara B., and Jonathan Haidt. "Witnessing Excellence in Action: The 'Other-Praising' Emotions of Elevation, Gratitude, and Admiration." *Journal of Positive Psychology* 4 (2009), 105–127.

Annas, Julia. *The Morality of Happiness*. Oxford: Oxford University Press, 1993.

———. *Intelligent Virtue*. Oxford: Oxford University Press, 2011.

Aristotle. *Manṭiq Arisṭū*, edited by ʿAbd al-Raḥmān Badawī. Beirut: Dār al-Qalam; Kuwait: Wakālat al-Maṭbūʿāt, 1980. 3 vols.

———. *The Arabic Version of the* Nicomachean Ethics, edited by Anna A. Akasoy and Alexander Fidora, with an introduction and annotated translation by Douglas M. Dunlop. Leiden: Brill, 2005.

Al-Ashʿarī, Abuʾl-Ḥasan. *Spotlights on the Confrontation of Deviance and Innovation/Kitāb al-Lumaʿ fiʾl-radd ʿalā ahl al-zaygh waʾl-bidaʿ*, edited by Ḥammūda Ghurāba. Cairo: Maṭbaʿat Miṣr, 1955.

Avicenna. *See* Ibn Sīnā.

Behrens-Abouseif, Doris. *Beauty in Arabic Culture*. Princeton, NJ: Markus Wiener, 1998.

Bergh, Simon Van Den. "The 'Love of God' in al-Ghazālī's *Vivification of Theology*." *Journal of Semitic Studies* 1 (1956), 305–321.

Black, Deborah L. "Aesthetics in Islamic Philosophy." In *Routledge Encyclopedia of Philosophy*, edited by Edward Craig, 75–79. London; New York: Routledge, 1998.

Brontë, Charlotte. *Jane Eyre*. New York; London: W. W. Norton & Company, 2001.

Casewit, Yousef. "Al-Ghazālī's Virtue Ethical Theory of the Divine Names: The Theological Underpinnings of the Doctrine of *Takhalluq* in *al-Maqṣad al-Asnā*." *Journal of Islamic Ethics* 4 (2020), 155–200.

Chittick, William C. "The Aesthetics of Islamic Ethics." In *Sharing Poetic Expressions: Beauty, Sublime, Mysticism in Islamic and Occidental Culture*, edited by Anna-Teresa Tymieniecka, 3–14. Dordrecht; New York: Springer, 2011.

Clewis, Robert R. *The Kantian Sublime and the Revelation of Freedom*. Cambridge: Cambridge University Press, 2009.

Cooper, David E. "Beautiful People, Beautiful Things." *British Journal of Aesthetics* 48 (2008), 247–260.

Daiber, Hans. "Griechische Ethik in islamischem Gewande: Das Beispiel von Rāġib al-Iṣfahānī (11. Jh.)." In *Historia Philosophiae Medii Aevi: Studien zur Geschichte der Philosophie des Mittelalters*, edited by Burkhard Mojsisch and Olaf Pluta, vol. 1, 181–192. Amsterdam; Philadelphia, PA: Grüner, 1992.

El Shamsy, Ahmed. "The Wisdom of God's Law: Two Theories." In *Islamic Law in Theory: Studies in Jurisprudence in Honor of Bernard Weiss*, edited by Robert Gleave and Kevin Reinhart, 19–37. Leiden: Brill, 2014.

Ernst, Carl. "Muḥammad as the Pole of Existence." In *The Cambridge Companion to Muḥammad*, edited by Jonathan E. Brockopp, 123–138. Cambridge: Cambridge University Press, 2010.

Ettinghausen, Richard. "Al-Ghazzālī on Beauty." In *Fine Arts of Islamic Civilization*, edited by Muhammad Abdul Jabbar Beg, 25–36. Cambridge: M. A. J. Beg, 2006.

Al-Fārābī, Abū Naṣr. *On the Perfect State/Mabādiʾ ārāʾ ahl al-madīna al-fāḍila*, translated by Richard Walzer. Oxford: Clarendon Press, 1985.

Frank, Richard M. *Al-Ghazālī and the Ashʿarite School*. Durham, NC; London: Duke University Press, 1994.

Galen. "Mukhtaṣar min Kitāb 'al-Akhlāq' li-Jālīnūs." In *Dirāsāt wa-nuṣūṣ fiʾl-falsafa waʾl-ʿulūm ʿinda al-ʿarab*, edited by ʿAbd al-Raḥmān Badawī, 190–211. Beirut: al-Muʾassasa al-ʿArabiyya liʾl-Dirāsāt waʾl-Nashr, 1981.

Garden, Kenneth. *The First Islamic Reviver: Abū Ḥāmid al-Ghazālī and His* Revival of the Religious Sciences. Oxford: Oxford University Press, 2014.

———. "Revisiting al-Ghazālī's Crisis Through his *Scale for Action* (*Mizān al-ʿAmal*)." In *Islam and Rationality: The Impact of al-Ghazālī*, vol. 1, edited by Georges Tamer, 207–228. Leiden: Brill, 2015.

Gaut, Berys. *Art, Emotion and Ethics*. Oxford: Oxford University Press, 2007.

Al-Ghazālī, Abū Ḥāmid. *The Quintessence of the Principles of Law/ Al-Mustaṣfā min ʿilm al-uṣūl*. Būlāq: al-Maṭbaʿa al-Amīriyya, 1904–1906. 2 vols.

———. *The Revival of the Religious Sciences/Iḥyāʾ ʿulūm al-dīn*. Cairo: Lajnat Nashr al-Thaqāfa al-Islāmiyya, 1937–38. 16 vols.

———. *Moderation in Belief/Al-Iqtiṣād fiʾl-iʿtiqād*, edited by Ibrahim Agâh Çubukçu and Hüseyin Atay. Ankara: Nur Matbaasi, 1962.

———. *The Scale of Action/Mīzān al-ʿamal*, edited by Sulaymān Dunyā. Cairo: Dār al-Maʿārif, 1964.

———. *The Deliverer from Error/Al-Munqidh min al-ḍalāl*, edited by Jamīl Ṣalībā and Kāmil ʿAyyād. 7th edn. Beirut: Dār al-Andalus, 1967.

———. *The Most Exalted Aim in Expounding God's Beautiful Names/Al-Maqṣad al-asnā fī sharḥ maʿānī asmāʾ Allāh al-ḥusnā*, edited by Fadlou A. Shehadi. Beirut: Dar El-Machreq, 1971.

Gianotti, Timothy J. *Al-Ghazālī's Unspeakable Doctrine of the Soul: Unveiling the Esoteric Psychology and Eschatology of the* Iḥyāʾ. Leiden: Brill, 2001.

Gonzalez, Valerie. *Beauty in Islam: Aesthetics in Islamic Art and Architecture.* London: I.B. Tauris, 2001.

Griffel, Frank. *Al-Ghazālī's Philosophical Theology.* New York: Oxford University Press, 2009.

———. "Al-Ghazālī's Use of "Original Human Disposition" (*Fiṭra*) and Its Background in the Teachings of al-Fārābī and Avicenna." *Muslim World* 102 (2012), 1–32.

Gutas, Dimitri. "Plato's *Symposion* in the Arabic Tradition." *Oriens* 31 (1988), 36–60.

———. "Platon. Tradition Arabe." In *Dictionnaire des Philosophes Antiques*, vol. Va, edited by Richard Goulet, 845–863. Paris: Centre National de la Recherche Scientifique, 2012.

Hacker, Peter. "Shame, Embarrassment, and Guilt." *Midwest Studies in Philosophy* 41 (2017), 202–224.

Haidt, Jonathan. "Elevation and the Positive Psychology of Morality." In *Flourishing: Positive Psychology and the Life Well-Lived*, edited by Corey L. M. Keyes and Jonathan Haidt, 275–280. Washington, DC: American Psychological Association, 2003.

Hillenbrand, Carole. "Some Aspects of al-Ghazālī's Views on Beauty." In *Gott ist schön und Er liebt die Schönheit (God is Beautiful and He Loves Beauty)*, edited by Alma Giese and J. Christoph Bürgel, 249–265. Bern: Peter Lang, 1994.

Hourani, George F. *Islamic Rationalism: The Ethics of ʿAbd al-Jabbār*. Oxford: Clarendon Press, 1971.

———. "A Revised Chronology of Ghazālī's Writings." *Journal of the American Oriental Society* 104 (1984), 289–302.

Hughes, Aaron. *The Texture of the Divine: Imagination in Medieval Islamic and Jewish Thought*. Bloomington; Indianapolis, IN: Indiana University Press, 2004.

Hume, David. *Treatise of Human Nature*, edited by L. A. Selby-Bigge, revised by P. H. Nidditch. 2nd edn. Oxford: Clarendon Press, 1978.

Ibn Manẓūr, Muḥammad ibn Mukarram. *The Arabic Tongue/Lisān al-'arab*. Beirut: Dār Ṣādir, 1955–1956. 15 vols.

Ibn Sīnā, Abū ʿAlī. "Risāla fiʾl-ʿishq." In *Jāmiʿ al-badāʾiʿ*, edited by Muḥyī al-Dīn Ṣabrī al-Kurdī, 68–91. Cairo: Maṭbaʿat al-Saʿāda, 1917.

———. *The Book of Salvation/Kitāb al-Najāt*, edited by Majid Fakhry. Beirut: Dār al-Āfāq al-Jadīda, 1985.

Irwin, Terence H. *The Development of Ethics*, vol. 1: *From Socrates to the Reformation.* Oxford: Oxford University Press, 2007.

———. "The Sense and Reference of *Kalon* in Aristotle." *Classical Philology* 105 (2010), 381–396.

Al-Qāḍī ʿIyāḍ, Abuʾl-Faḍl ibn Mūsā. *The Curative Knowledge of the Claims of the Chosen Prophet/Al-Shifāʾ bi-taʿrīf ḥuqūq al-muṣṭafā*, edited by ʿAlī Muḥammad al-Bajāwī. Beirut: Dār al-Kitāb al-ʿArabī, 1984. 2 vols.

Janssens, Jules. "Al-Ghazālī's *Mīzān al-ʿAmal*: An Ethical Summa Based on Ibn Sīnā and al-Rāghib al-Iṣfahānī." In *Islamic Thought in the Middle Ages: Studies in Text, Transmission and Translation in Honour of Hans Daiber*, edited by Anna Akasoy and Wim Raven, 123–137. Leiden: Brill, 2008.

Kahn, Charles. "Pre-Platonic Ethics." In *Ethics—Companions to Ancient Thought*, vol. 4, edited by Stephen Everson, 27–48. Cambridge: Cambridge University Press, 1998.

Kamali, Mohammad Hashim. *Shari'ah Law: An Introduction.* Oxford: Oneworld, 2008.

Kant, Immanuel. *Critique of the Power of Judgment*, translated by Paul Guyer and Eric Matthews. Cambridge: Cambridge University Press, 2000.

Kidd, Ian James. "Beauty, Virtue, and Religious Exemplars." *Religious Studies* 53 (2017), 171–181.

———. "Admiration, Attraction and the Aesthetics of Exemplarity." *Journal of Moral Education* 48 (2019), 369–380.

Kosman, Aryeh. "Beauty and the Good: Situating the *Kalon*." *Classical Philology* 105 (2010), 341–357.

Kristjánsson, Kristján. "Emotions Targeting Moral Exemplarity: Making Sense of the Logical Geography of Admiration, Emulation and Elevation." *Theory and Research in Education* 15 (2017), 20–37.

Kukkonen, Taneli. "The Good, the Beautiful and the True: Aesthetical Issues in Islamic Philosophy." *Studia Orientalia* 111 (2011), 87–103.

———. "Al-Ghazālī on the Origins of Ethics." *Numen* 63 (2016), 271–298.

Leaman, Oliver. *Islamic Aesthetics*. Edinburgh: Edinburgh University Press, 2004.

Madelung, Wilferd. "Ar-Rāġib al-Iṣfahānī und die Ethik al-Ġazālīs." In *Islamwissenschaftliche Abhandlungen Fritz Meier zum sechzigsten Geburtstag*, edited by Richard Gramlich, 152–163. Wiesbaden: Steiner, 1974.

Mahmoud, Samir. "Beauty and Aesthetics in Classical Islamic Thought: An Introduction." *Kalam Journal* 1 (2018), 7–21.

Mānkdīm Shashdīw, Aḥmad ibn al-Ḥusayn. *[Taʿlīq] Sharḥ al-Uṣūl al-khamsa*, edited by ʿAbd al-Karīm ʿUthmān. Cairo: Maktabat Wahba, 1965.

Matravers, Derek. *Fiction and Narrative*. Oxford: Oxford University Press, 2014.

McGinn, Colin. *Ethics, Evil, and Fiction*. Oxford: Oxford University Press, 1999.

Mohamed, Yasien. "The Ethical Philosophy of al-Rāghib al-Iṣfahānī." *Journal of Islamic Studies* 6 (1995), 51–75.

———. "The Ethics of Education: al-Iṣfahānī's *al-Dharīʿa* as a Source of Inspiration for al-Ghazālī's *Mīzān al-ʿAmal*." *Muslim World* 101 (2011), 633–657.

Murata, Kazuyo. *Beauty in Sufism: The Teachings of Rūzbihān Baqlī*. Albany, NY: State University of New York Press, 2017.

Murtaḍā al-Zabīdī, Muḥammad ibn Muḥammad. *The Bridal Crown from the Gems of the Dictionary/Tāj al-ʿArūs min jawāhir al-Qāmūs*, edited by various editors. Kuwait: Maṭbaʿat Ḥukūmat al-Kuwayt, 1965–2001. 40 vols.

Nietzsche, Friedrich. *Twilight of the Idols and the Anti-Christ*, translated by R. J. Hollingdale. London: Penguin, 1990.

———. *Untimely Meditations*, edited by Daniel Breazeale and translated by R. J. Hollingdale. Cambridge: Cambridge University Press, 1997.

Nussbaum, Martha C. *Upheavals of Thought: The Intelligence of Emotions*. Cambridge; New York: Cambridge University Press, 2001.

Paris, Panos. "On Form, and the Possibility of Moral Beauty." *Metaphilosophy* 49 (2018), 711–729.

———. "The Empirical Case for Moral Beauty." *Australasian Journal of Philosophy* 96 (2018), 642–656.

———. "Moral Beauty and Education." *Journal of Moral Education* 48 (2019), 395–411.

Plato. *Symposium*, translated by Reginald E. Allen. New Haven, CT: Yale University Press, 1993.

Plotinus. *Plotinus Apud Arabes/Aflūṭīn ʿinda al-ʿarab*, edited by ʿAbd al-Raḥmān Badawī. Cairo: Maktabat al-Nahḍa al-Miṣriyya, 1955.

Puerta Vílchez, José Miguel. *Aesthetics in Arabic Thought from Pre-Islamic Arabia through al-Andalus,* translated by Consuelo López-Morillas. Leiden; Boston, MA: Brill, 2017.

Radford, Colin. "How Can We Be Moved by the Fate of Anna Karenina?" *Proceedings of the Aristotelian Society, Supplementary Volumes* 49 (1975), 67–80.

Al-Rāghib al-Iṣfahānī, Abuʾl-Qāsim ibn Muḥammad. *An Exposition of the Obscure Terms of the Qurʾan/Mufradāt fī gharīb al-Qurʾān*, edited by Ṣafwān ʿAdnān Dawūdī. 4th edn. Damascus: Dār al-Qalam; Beirut: al-Dār al-Shāmiyya, 2009.

Al-Rāzī, Fakhr al-Dīn. *The Keys to the Unseen/Mafātīḥ al-ghayb*, Beirut: Dār al-Fikr, 1981. 32 vols.

Rosenthal, Franz. *Four Essays on Art and Literature in Islam*. Leiden: Brill, 1971.

Schimmel, Anne-Marie. *And Mohammed is His Messenger: The Veneration of the Prophet in Islamic Piety*. Chapel Hill, NC: London: University of North Carolina Press, 1985.

Schopenhauer, Arthur. *The World as Will and Representation*, translated by E. F. J. Payne. New York: Dover Publications, 1966. 2 vols.

Scruton, Roger. *Art and Imagination: A Study in the Philosophy of Mind*. South Bend, IN: St Augustine's Press, 1998.

Sherif, Mohamed Ahmed. *Ghazālī's Theory of Virtue*. Albany, NY: State University of New York Press, 1975.

Sidgwick, Henry. *The Methods of Ethics*. 7th edn. Indianapolis, IN: Hackett, 1981.

Al-Tawḥīdī, Abū Ḥayyān, and Abū ʿAlī Miskawayh. *The Philosopher Responds: An Intellectual Correspondence From the Tenth Century*, edited by Bilal Orfali and Maurice A. Pomerantz and translated by Sophia Vasalou and James E. Montgomery. New York: New York University Press, 2019.

Watt, W. Montgomery. "The Authenticity of the Works Attributed to al-Ghazālī." *Journal of the Royal Asiatic Society of Great Britain and Ireland* 1/2 (1952), 24–45.

———. *Muslim Intellectual: A Study of al-Ghazālī*. Edinburgh: Edinburgh University Press, 1963.

———. "Al-Ghazālī." In *Encyclopaedia of Islam*, edited by P. Bearman, Th. Bianquis, C. E. Bosworth, E. van Donzel, and W. P. Heinrichs. 2nd edn. Consulted online on 23 August 2020: http://dx.doi.org/10.1163/1573-3912_islam_COM_0233

Wensinck, Arent J. *La Pensée de Ghazzālī*. Paris: Adrien-Maisonneuve, 1940.

Williams, Bernard. *Shame and Necessity*. Berkeley, LA: University of California Press, 1993.

Wittgenstein, Ludwig. *Philosophical Investigations*, edited by Peter M. S. Hacker and Joachim Schulte, translated by G. E. M. Anscombe, Peter M. S. Hacker, and Joachim Schulte. 4th rev. edn. Chichester: Wiley-Blackwell, 2009.

Vasalou, Sophia. *Moral Agents and their Deserts: The Character of Muʿtazilite Ethics*. Princeton, NJ: Princeton University Press, 2008.

———. *Ibn Taymiyya's Theological Ethics*. New York: Oxford University Press, 2016.

———. *Virtues of Greatness in the Arabic Tradition*. Oxford: Oxford University Press, 2019.

———. "Admiration, Emulation, and the Description of Character." *Journal of Aesthetic Education* 54 (2020), 47–69.

———. "Virtue and the Law in al-Ghazālī's Ethics." In *Islamic Ethics as Educational Discourse: Thought and Impact of the Classical Muslim Thinker Miskawayh*, edited by Sebastian Günther and Yassir El Jamouhi. Tübingen: Mohr Siebeck, 2021.

———. "Does al-Ghazālī Have a Theory of Virtue?" In *Mysticism and Ethics in Islam*, edited by Bilal Orfali, Mohammed Rustom, and Atif Khalil. Beirut: American University of Beirut Press, forthcoming.

———. "Ethics as Medicine: Moral Therapy, Expertise, and Practical Reasoning in al-Ghazālī's Ethics." *Archiv für Geschichte der Philosophie* (2021). https://doi.org/10.1515/agph-2020-5006

Zagzebski, Linda T. *Exemplarist Moral Theory*. New York: Oxford University Press, 2017.

Zangwill, Nick. *The Metaphysics of Beauty*. Ithaca, NY; London: Cornell University Press, 2001.

Zargar, Cyrus Ali. *Sufi Aesthetics: Beauty, Love, and the Human Form in Ibn Arabi and ʿIraqi*. Columbia, SC: University of South Carolina Press, 2011.

Index